Built by
BLACKS

Built by BLACKS

African American Architecture and Neighborhoods in Richmond

Selden Richardson

Editor and Photographer Maurice Duke, PhD

THE
History
PRESS

Published by The History Press
Charleston, SC 29403
www.historypress.net

Cover design by Marshall Hudson.

All images courtesy of Maurice Duke unless otherwise noted.

Originally published 2007
The History Press edition 2008
Second printing 2011

ISBN 978-1-5402-1868-1

Library of Congress Cataloging-in-Publication Data

Richardson, Selden.
Built by Blacks : African American architecture and neighborhoods in Richmond / Selden Richardson ; editor
and photographer, Maurice Duke.
p. cm.
"The Alliance to Conserve Old Richmond Neighborhoods, Richmond, Virginia."
Includes bibliographical references and index.
ISBN 978-1-5402-1868-1
1. African American architecture--Virginia--Richmond. 2. African Americans--Virginia--Richmond--Social
conditions. 3. Richmond (Va.)--Buildings, structures, etc. 4. Richmond (Va.)--Social conditions. I. Duke,
Maurice. II. Alliance to Conserve Old Richmond Neighborhoods. III. Title.
NA735.R5R53 2008
720.89'960730755451--dc22
2008007274

Contents

Illustrations

Preface

This book traces its origins to a visit to the offices of the Alliance to Conserve Old Richmond Neighborhoods (ACORN) on a rainy Friday afternoon in late 2002 by two frantic residents of the Manchester area of south Richmond. The two warned that a small cottage on Commerce Road was scheduled to be demolished the following Monday. As evidence of the significance of the structure, they presented a copy of the original deed showing the conveyance of the house immediately after the Civil War to a black woman, who signed the document with an "X."

The ACORN staff felt that the woman, named Emily Winfree, may have once been a slave. The architecture of the house itself echoed a typical design of a slave quarters: a single-story frame dwelling of two rooms separated by a dividing wall and a central chimney serving both rooms. Initial research revealed that this was the lone surviving structure in what had been a thriving African American community in lower Manchester. In modern Richmond there is a scarcity of brick versions of this kind of home, let alone a frame example. ACORN saw the rescue of the Winfree Cottage as clearly in line with its mission as an advocate for old Richmond neighborhoods and took steps to avert the imminent demolition of the house.

The Richmond Slave Trail Commission assisted in the rescue by arranging to relocate the house to a vacant lot owned by the city at Seventeenth and Broad Streets. The crisis having passed, ACORN researchers began to investigate Winfree and her house. A remarkable story was revealed, opening a window onto little-known aspects of antebellum cultural history. The cottage did indeed belong to a former slave and was the sole survivor of the neighborhood she knew. Her onetime owner, and the father of her five children, purchased the home for her for $800 in 1866. Winfree raised her children in one room of the tiny house while sometimes renting out the other room to make ends meet.

Researchers discovered Emily Winfree's prominent gravesite in Maury Cemetery in south Richmond and her photograph in the collections of the Library of Virginia. They studied the complicated and interwoven genealogy of the Winfree families, black and white. In this process of discovery, Winfree's story unfolded and became emblematic of the experiences of thousands of black Richmonders who populated the city before and after the Civil War.

The Slave Trail Commission plans to restore the Winfree Cottage and make it a focal point on the Slave Trail through Shockoe Bottom (as Shockoe Valley is generally known today).

Ironically, research revealed that the lot on Broad Street to which the cottage was moved was the location of a now demolished slave jail owned by Silas Omohundro. Nearby stood the notorious Lumpkin's Jail (also demolished). Owner Robert Lumpkin lived with his former slave mistress and their children in a house on the site and married her after the Civil War. The Lumpkin's Jail site was significant even after the Civil War, when Lumpkin's widow leased the jail to a school for blacks that evolved into Virginia Union University.

Directly to the north of the proposed site of the Winfree Cottage is the Burial Ground for Negroes, the burial place for an unknown number of enslaved blacks whose existence was forgotten over the years. Built upon at various times during the last 150 years, the cemetery is today a featureless paved parking lot.

The Winfree Cottage, like the Burial Ground for Negroes, came to symbolize the state of African American history in Richmond and the condition of the stage upon which

Emily Winfree raised five children in one room of this tiny cottage. The structure was saved by the Alliance to Conserve Old Richmond Neighborhoods. Plans call for it to be incorporated into a visitors' center.

generations of Richmond blacks enacted their lives. The exploration of these places and their present unfortunate state of decay and neglect underscores the need for more aggressive preservation and a more inclusive understanding of the city's history.

The dramatic contrast between historic sites has never been as vivid as when seen in the condition of the city's neglected black cemeteries. Great strides have been taken recently in preserving the Barton Heights burying ground (actually several adjacent African American cemeteries), but the contrast between what was once the premier African American cemetery called Evergreen and Richmond's famous Hollywood Cemetery for whites is appalling.

Likewise, the documentation of African American life in general and the experience of the black slave in particular are largely missing from the record, despite a plethora of writing on Richmond's history. Only recently has this void begun to be filled. Two noteworthy works on the subject are Midori Takagi's 1999 *Rearing Wolves to Our Own Destruction* and Gregg D. Kimball's *American City, Southern Place: A Cultural History of Antebellum Richmond* published in 2000. Jeffrey Ruggles's *The Unboxing of Henry Brown*, published in 2003, describes the world of antebellum Richmond and an escape from it by an exceptional African American.

A new examination of early black Richmond is demanded, if only by the sheer number of African Americans who lived in the city or were marketed at a Richmond slave trading facility and passed from there to hard labor in the Deep South. These numbers are staggering, compared to what is known of their lives. As an example, just before the Civil War there were some fourteen thousand free and enslaved black residents in the city, compared to a total population of approximately twenty-four thousand. The presence of over half of the population was noted only when it was deemed necessary to control or discipline African Americans. These otherwise faceless thousands only appear fleetingly on police blotters or reward notices for their return to bondage, on sales manifests and as victims of the infamous Black Codes, which were engineered to further constrict the lives and activities of Richmonders of color. Early nineteenth-century African American cemetery records preserve the names of a few prominent black Richmond residents.

This historical void became more apparent as research undertaken by ACORN expanded. Many more questions arose than answers. How many African American entrepreneurs built the engine that drove what became known as the "Black Wall Street" of Richmond, and who were the architects, contractors and artisans who built the homes and churches, halls and stores of the segregated city? How much of that built environment remained and where were the stories of the struggle to construct them? Much of this history has been lost, but many of the buildings in which the fight for success and freedom, civil rights and dignity occurred remain despite the destruction generated in the name of urban renewal and "progress." It is the hope of ACORN, its staff and volunteers that this book will begin the process of filling that considerable void.

Due to time and other constraints, this book is not a complete history. Nor does it chronicle the story of post–World War II public housing, a history with far-reaching architectural and social consequences for Richmond. Much remains to be written about this

Richmond slave Emily Winfree bore five children by her owner David Winfree. She raised them in a two-room cottage, one room of which she rented out to make ends meet. *Courtesy Library of Virginia.*

Emily Winfree's tombstone in Maury Cemetery.

city. For example, almost every one of Richmond's African American churches has its own history of determination and endurance.

A comprehensive and citywide program of oral histories conducted with older members of these churches would yield valuable information about life in Richmond that otherwise will soon be lost. Many prominent black Richmonders remain to be identified and given places of significance and the buildings they built and lived in recalled and recorded.

The story of Richmond's past, as evidenced by the recent archaeological explorations in Shockoe Valley, is still being uncovered. In addition, the loss of Richmond's architectural fabric, from iconic downtown offices and stores to humble bungalows, is being compounded constantly.

Even the most modest of these homes, businesses and churches in our old neighborhoods is a repository of the collective memories of generations of Richmonders and each is an artifact of its historical moment. An honest and complete story of the city is impossible without the preservation of these areas of the city. It is our hope that this book will heighten awareness and appreciation for these places where Richmond's African Americans lived and worked, worshipped and mourned, and in the end, persevered.

Acknowledgements

A number of people interested in the preservation of Richmond's long, colorful and sometimes troubling history have been instrumental in the writing of this book. Although many of them worked behind the scenes, they nevertheless provided valuable information, ideas and research that helped form this narrative as it progressed over the months. Board members, staff and volunteers associated with the Alliance to Conserve Old Richmond Neighborhoods (ACORN) provided valuable assistance, and Jennie Dotts, executive director of ACORN, coordinated the project.

Melinda Skinner set the project in motion with an inquiry to a publisher. Teresa Roane, former director of archives and curator of photographs at the Valentine Richmond History Center (and now the library manager at the Museum of the Confederacy), provided invaluable research, guidance and scholarship—particularly regarding antebellum Richmond. Barbara Swift Smith, formerly with the Library of Virginia, and Denise Lester, with the Burial Ground Society of Virginia, brought vivid and human dimensions to architectural research through their genealogical expertise. David Herring offered not only ideas but also advice in the formative stage of the project. He and Mindy Tanner served as project coordinators for the book.

Architectural historian Kim Chen, archivist Vince Brooks and researchers Michael Dodson, Matthew Cushman and Ronald Mitchell brought details to light that helped to put a human face on the story of Richmond's African American experience. Dixon Kerr offered much insight, and his carpentry skills helped to secure the Winfree Cottage.

Benjamin Ross, church historian for Sixth Mt. Zion Baptist Church, answered questions concerning emphasis and approach to materials. Gregg Kimball and Jeffrey Ruggles, knowledgeable Richmond authors and historians, helped straighten out seemingly disparate facts in Richmond's long story. Staff members of the Valentine Richmond History Center, the Virginia Historical Society, the Library of Virginia, the Black History Museum and Cultural Center and the Chesterfield Historical Society all provided valuable assistance.

Members of the Richmond Slave Trail Commission, particularly its chairperson, the Honorable Delores McQuinn, gave encouragement at the outset, as did William Reinhart. Thomas Tyler Potterfield Jr. provided essential research and generously made his working files available for the project. Charlie Finley of Verbatim Editing did the final checking and proofreading.

Many others have also had a hand in the writing of this book, either through advice or encouragement. They include Charles Bethea, Muriel Miller Branch, Dr. Charles Brownell, Arnold Henderson, Florence Henderson, Robinson Horne, Dr. Francis Foster, Mary Sands ("Sandy") Satterwhite, Dr. Philip Schwarz, James Sheffield, Stephen Slipek, Ronald Stallings, Kathleen Valentine, Laverne B. Smith, Ray Boone and Celia Suggs.

The Virginia Foundation for the Humanities provided essential funds to support development of the book, and an anonymous gift made its publication possible. In addition, contributions given to save the Winfree Cottage should be acknowledged, as the cottage was the catalyst for the research that led to the book: Walter M. Dotts III; Zayde R. Dotts; Edmund A. Rennolds Jr.; Mary Z. Zeugner and the Elmwood Fund; Dr. Joseph C. Parker and Ernest and Melinda Skinner, in memory of Mary Elizabeth Woodfin Crute; the Roller-Bottimore Foundation; and the Windsor Foundation. Additional funding came from Muriel Miller Branch and Meta and John Braymer.

The City of Richmond donated land and services for relocating the Winfree Cottage, thereby saving it from destruction at the eleventh hour. Taylor and Parrish Inc., on whose property the cottage was located, donated the cottage to ACORN when notified of its significance. Jim Matyko of Expert Movers responded cheerfully and immediately to ACORN's request for help in moving the house. On an early Sunday several autumns ago, Jim transported the cottage on a trailer from its perch in Manchester to the site of a now-vanished slave jail in Shockoe Bottom, spurring an investigation that resulted in an intensive focus on the experience of Richmond's slave trade.

Special thanks go to Brett Hosier who, late one Friday afternoon in October 2002, appeared at the door of ACORN with a copy of the original deed for the ramshackle cottage scheduled for demolition the following Monday. He and G. William Thomas, as president of the Manchester Civic Association, helped piece together the remarkable story of former slave Emily Winfree and her complex relationship with the family that once owned her—a relationship symbolized by the cottage and its subsequent relocation to the heart of Richmond's slave trading center. ACORN's talented intern, Gretchen Goodman, laid out this book and helped edit it, bringing to bear on it the insights of a generation far removed from the subject. Dr. Maurice Duke (author of books and articles on Virginia history and slavery) added immeasurably to ACORN's understanding of the importance of the Winfree Cottage and its ability to illustrate how people of different races lived, worked and interacted in nineteenth-century Richmond. Dr. Duke contributed countless volunteer hours to the project—scouring archives and libraries for written documents and visual images—thus helping to fill in elusive details. In the end, he served as manuscript editor, photographer and photo editor. Thanks also to Dr. Duke's wife, Anne Duke, for her keen proofreading skills and encouraging advice.

I'd especially like to thank my wife Karri for her love and support during the research and writing of this book.

The rescue of the humble Winfree Cottage fired the imaginations of ACORN staff members, trustees, donors and volunteers who thought that a book about Richmond's African American neighborhoods would illuminate a neglected part of the city's history.

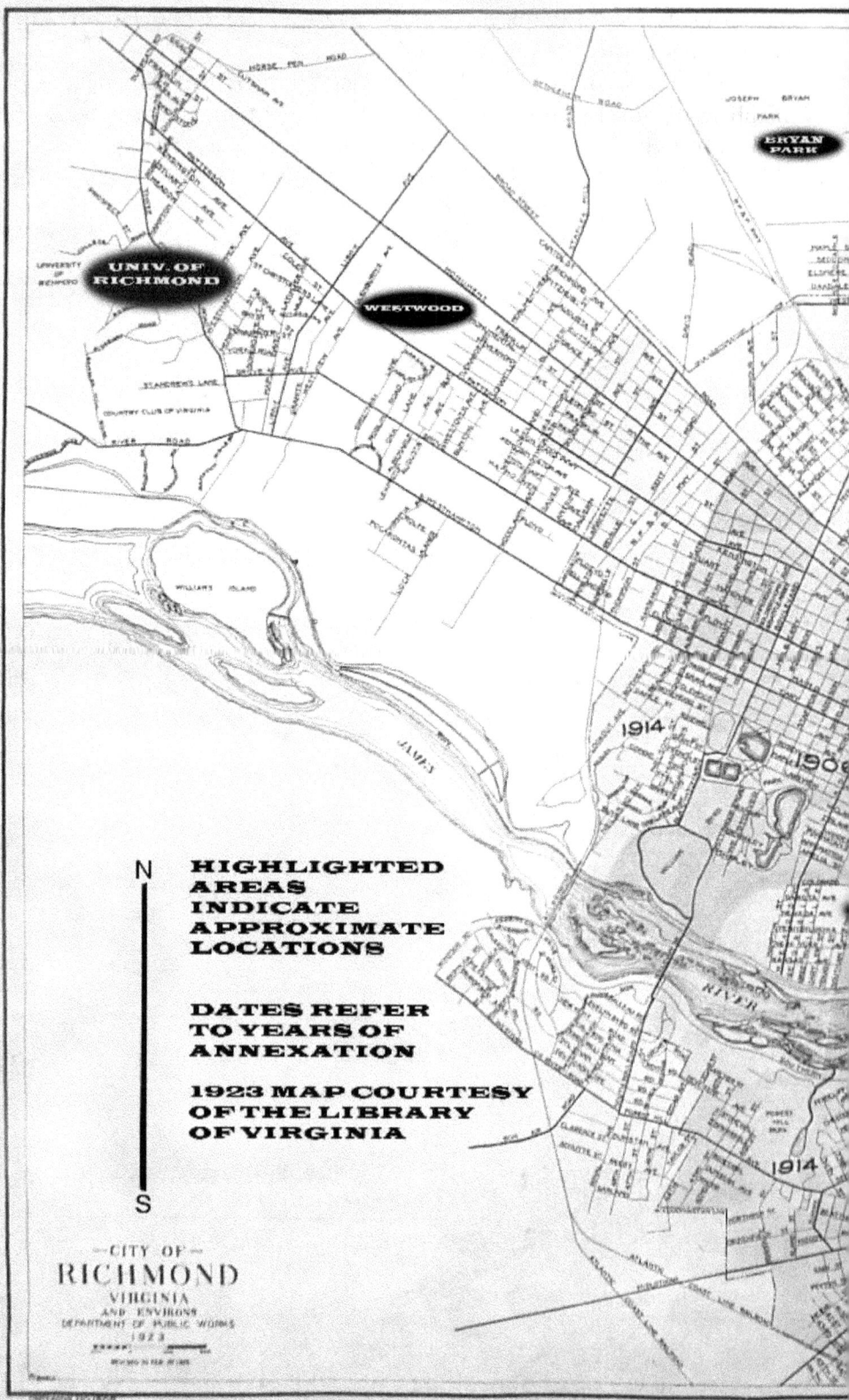

HIGHLIGHTED
AREAS
INDICATE
APPROXIMATE
LOCATIONS

DATES REFER
TO YEARS OF
ANNEXATION

1923 MAP COURTESY
OF THE LIBRARY
OF VIRGINIA

N

S

—CITY OF—
RICHMOND
VIRGINIA
AND ENVIRONS
DEPARTMENT OF PUBLIC WORKS
1923

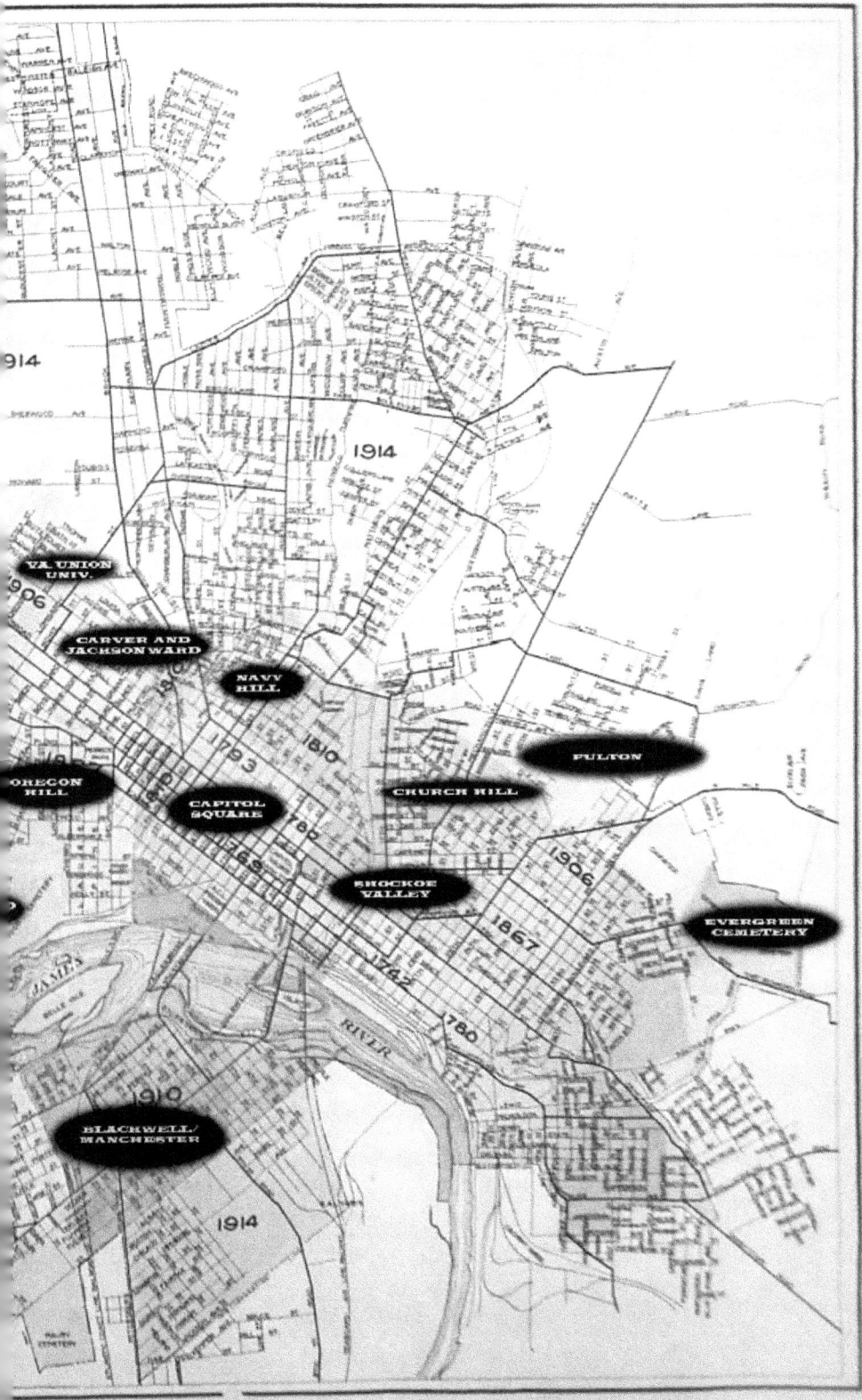

VA. UNION UNIV.

CARVER AND JACKSON WARD

NAVY HILL

OREGON HILL

CAPITOL SQUARE

CHURCH HILL

FULTON

SHOCKOE VALLEY

EVERGREEN CEMETERY

BLACKWELL/ MANCHESTER

1914

1906

1793

1810

782

768

1906

1867

1742

780

1910

1914

JAMES

RIVER

1

The Beginning
Early Slavery and Early Buildings

"It was a hovel built...of bricks and mud."
—*Samuel Mordecai*

T he falls of the James River, where the city of Richmond stands, were first noted by an early expedition only days after the landing of English colonists in Virginia in 1607. Blocked by the roaring expanse of broken water ahead of them, the Englishmen turned their craft ashore and parlayed with a group of Native Americans at a site slightly east of today's downtown Richmond.[1] Captain Christopher Newport and his men had come to the head of navigation. From this point on, the vast, unknown expanse of the North American continent stretched out toward the west.

All too soon the reality of the Virginia countryside became clear to the new arrivals. There was no gold to be found scattered in the pine woods and no groves of exotic spices to be harvested. The potential of the drop in the river and how it might be harnessed, combined with the geographic obstacles thwarting westward movement, would eventually delineate much of the character and the success of the city of Richmond.

The exploration and the knowledge of what lay beyond the falls, as well as the importation of thousands of people, black and white, would come in time. But initial attempts to colonize the area where the Shockoe Valley met the James repeatedly failed. The settlement at the falls was abandoned in 1609 under pressure from the natives. Native American attacks in 1622 and 1644 repeatedly caused the tide of exploration to recede.[2] For years the site was left to the river, the woods and the natives while the English retreated and regrouped. Dreams of finding a passage to the Orient through the rivers of Virginia, long a goal of European explorers, also quickly faded with the exploration of the rivers of Tidewater Virginia. More pragmatic plans were made to take advantage of the commercial potential of the site at the falls of the James.

Typical of the new Virginians, who viewed the area for its commercial and agricultural uses, was the Byrd family. The Byrds saw Virginia as having enormous potential for more prosaic development than gold and spices. They correctly identified agriculture and industry as the ways to wring a family fortune from the trackless woods and fields of Tidewater Virginia.

The financial successes of William Byrd I (1652–1704) and his son serve as a case in point, as both men were instrumental in bringing English entrepreneurship to the area. Father and son seized every opportunity available in the Virginia colony and established a commercial empire that encompassed thousands of acres. Indeed, the senior Byrd was characterized as

> *a model of the aspiring planter, taking advantage of every opportunity to acquire land, trade with Indians, buy and sell Indian and African slaves, produce and market tobacco, and compete for patronage offices in the colonial government.*[3]

As the tiny hamlet at the falls of the James developed, Byrd's son William Byrd II (1674–1744), both a slave owner and part owner of a slave-transporting ship, was responsible for officially founding Richmond and giving it and the nearby city of Petersburg their names. He also was a civic leader (as was expected of the gentry) and one of the leading intellectuals and writers in early America.

Byrd and his contemporaries grew up in Virginia in the late seventeenth and early eighteenth centuries in the era of indentured servitude. Early in the life of the colony the majority of the laborers in fields and farms owned by the leading Virginia families were white Englishmen and Englishwomen, often of modest means, who had agreed to labor for a certain period in exchange for passage to the colonies and a start in life in the New World. These individuals ran the gamut from unskilled laborers to carpenters, shipbuilders, craftspeople, teachers and the like. Soon, however, their numbers diminished as blacks (in effect indentured for life) were rapidly, if unwillingly, assuming the duties formerly performed by the indentured workers.

The first recorded appearance of Africans in the New World occurred in the summer of 1619 when a Dutch ship arrived in Jamestown, approximately fifty miles downriver from present-day Richmond. Although controversy surrounds the early Africans' status, it appears they arrived subject to a type of indenture rather than as slaves. However, that status was soon to change.[4] Enslaved Africans quickly became the primary workforce in the colony.

The most significant early influx of Africans to the Virginia colony occurred during the late seventeenth and early eighteenth centuries. Soon they had assumed almost the entire burden of the physical labor needed to keep the colony functioning. Indeed, their numbers quickly surpassed those of the white indentured servants. With the increasing population of blacks in the Virginia colony, the English courts reinterpreted and tightened the laws centering on slavery. Anecdotal evidence of legal decisions demonstrates that the laws of the colony relegated Africans and African Americans to the status of permanent servitude. By 1705, the disparate laws affecting only blacks were codified into the first slave code of Virginia, ushering in the system of permanent slavery, grounded in law, which was not to be voided until the conclusion of the Civil War some 160 years later.[5] By 1680, African slaves performed almost all the manual labor. Between 1680 and 1750 the ratio of blacks increased by 34 percent. This coincided with a decline of white immigrants willing to work under an indenture

William Byrd II of Westover (1674–1744) was a planter, businessman and colonial leader. He was also part owner of a slave ship that transported Africans to Virginia. Byrd founded and named the cities of Richmond and Petersburg and was one of the major intellectuals in the American colonies prior to the American Revolution. *Courtesy Library of Virginia.*

contract. Meanwhile, increased production of tobacco and other labor-intensive crops drove a demand for more laborers.[6]

As Virginia went from an English colony to an American state, the nature of the slavery system changed markedly. In the closing decades of the eighteenth century, Richmond became a clearing station for the slave-selling business, bringing thousands of people of color to the rapidly growing town. So great was the number of these American-born blacks that in 1778 Virginia passed a law forbidding further importations of Africans, closing a transatlantic business that had flourished since the 1600s. In 1808, the United States government passed laws that forbade the importation of Africans in the entire country. Virginia then became, through natural increase, one of America's largest slaveholding states. Virginia's central location on the mid-Atlantic seaboard gave rise to its prominence as a hub for the trafficking of slaves. Through their forced labor, African American slaves played a major role in shaping the physical appearance and moral structure of Richmond long before it was incorporated as a city in 1782. From the earliest times, life for blacks in Richmond differed from that of their plantation counterparts by virtue of Richmond's urban setting, however rudimentary. The urban setting changed as the city expanded its boundaries and grew in affluence. Rural and urban slave experiences differed because living and working conditions in the city dictated closer interaction between the races than isolated rural environments allowed.

A large measure of Richmond's early power and influence was based on the industrial and service populations of enslaved blacks (a comparatively small number of free blacks toiled in the city's factories and homes). The black population furnished much of the unskilled labor that dug Richmond's canals, constructed buildings and manned the growing number of heavy industries clustered along the banks of the James River. At the same time, more African Americans rose beyond menial labor and developed skills as artisans and craftsmen. This was particularly true among free blacks who took advantage of the urban setting to earn money as skilled workers and purchase their freedom, becoming entrepreneurs and forging their own paths out of bondage.

The industrial base, fueled by slave labor, soon made Richmond not only the logical center of political power in the Southern states but also, at a later time, a military objective of supreme importance. Eventually, the exhaustion of soil by tobacco farming forced many slave owners to divest themselves of their chattel, while surplus slaves from Tidewater, Piedmont and western areas of the state were routinely sent to Richmond to be sold or leased. Thus the city grew into a major slave export center, from which slaves were sold to other areas of the country. During the Civil War, Richmond was important not only as the political capital of the Confederacy, but also as the economic engine that drove the economy of the upper South. The concept of attacking the economic as well as the military resources of a nation was refined during the Civil War. The fall of Richmond and the destruction of the slave-driven manufacturing center within its defenses validated this concept and delivered a fatal blow to the Confederacy, a blow from which it could not possibly recover.

Because the operation of the early slave trade is largely undocumented, we must rely on disparate evidence to understand the lives of the city's earliest African Americans as they related to and existed in the architectural record of the city. Few of the physical structures associated with enslaved African Americans remain. The surviving architecture includes factories, warehouses and those substantial living quarters associated with wealthy owners. The architectural record of slavery is meager because of poor construction, inferior materials and efforts after the Civil War to erase the vestiges of the institution.

It is a fair assumption that William Byrd II's trading settlement on the north bank of the James would not have been architecturally impressive given the primitive conditions overall. One description of the early Virginia countryside of the seventeenth century paints a depressing picture of "a winding dirt road, stump-packed fields, rail fences, tiny buildings, medieval and dilapidated in appearance, and the ever-present woods."[7] Only the presence of a small fortification and several of Byrd's warehouse and store buildings hinted at the city to come. Stone and brick construction came later, when commercial success inspired confidence in the future.

The construction of these early warehouses was done with a technique now called "earthfast," meaning that the buildings were constructed without masonry piers to hold the wooden members off the ground. Instead, the posts and sills were laid directly onto the soil, and this resulted in a highly impermanent building type, also known as the "Virginia House." Constructing buildings in this manner made them highly susceptible to the dampness of Virginia weather, and termites began to attack the wood almost immediately.[8] Because of this, the built environment of early Virginia for both blacks and whites has largely vanished.

The first blacks to arrive in the hamlet that would eventually become Richmond were probably housed in primitive structures that sheltered them from the weather. The more fortunate may have lived in quarters vacated by the increasingly fewer indentured servants, but evidence of the lives of the earliest black Richmonders in architectural records is nonexistent.[9] With the passage of time, a dormitory-style housing emerged and eventually gave way to more private structures as slave families and the town began to grow. This, in turn, dictated the need for separate and largely racially segregated housing. In the context of the settlement later called "Shacco's,"[10] it became necessary for slave owners to have laborers nearby in individual buildings in what was becoming an increasingly urban setting. The proximity of slave housing was for both security and efficiency, and it meant that blacks were under increased surveillance while tending to their work. This is in contrast to rural slaves, since those in rural environments lived in quarters at some distance from the main house.

The principal buildings of Richmond at the time of the American Revolution are shown on a map that illustrated a military engagement in 1781. They appear as a scattering of thirty-one structures on both sides of what is now Shockoe Valley, roughly laid out on a grid pattern. A few buildings marked "warehouses" are outside of town. For blacks and whites alike, the valley split by Shockoe Creek contained their residences, places of employment and commerce.

As shown on the 1781 map, on the south side of the James River stood the industrial buildings of the town of Manchester. Originally known as Rocky Ridge, Manchester is

An extensive rock field and heavy vegetation kept the English from proceeding up the James River beyond the present-day site of Richmond. Thus, William Byrd II established the tiny village at this site, which was called the "falls."

depicted as a tiny hamlet on a British officer's military map, with only eight buildings loosely grouped where this part of south Richmond stands today.[11]

A view of Richmond a year later shows it to be a town of more than 1,000 inhabitants. Of these, almost half were black; of the 468 blacks, 40 were free. It is also noteworthy that there was little discrimination as far as where blacks and whites lived, with the population being evenly scattered among the residential areas of the small town.[12] Almost all the houses were of frame construction and were "not large nor [were] they in themselves of a handsome appearance," recalled David Schöpf, who visited Richmond in 1783.[13]

With the loss over the years of a vast majority of the buildings that were home to African Americans in antebellum Richmond, even descriptions of these structures are rare. Indeed, so much of the pre–Civil War housing stock of whites and blacks alike has been lost that what is left consists largely of the finest, most durable homes. Thousands of the humble houses that sheltered both slave and slave owner have disappeared, and the architectural record of generations of Richmonders has been lost.

Regarding the Richmond cityscape in antebellum Richmond, one historian notes:

> The vast majority of slaves were housed in the homes of their owners. However, if a slave was expertly skilled, he might be hired out and allowed to live in the house or shop of his employer. There was, then, little architectural difference between the living quarters of blacks and whites as both groups occupied the same spaces. Slaves might be kept separate from the family in an attic area or in a room at the back of the kitchen, but there was rarely an external sign that slaves lived in a particular house.[14]

Those African Americans who could not find housing on the floor of a white person's house, or in a garret or outbuilding, had to rely on their own meager resources to find living accommodations. A glimpse of the kind and quality of these structures can be found in a description of the dwelling of an African American tooth puller named Peter Hawkins. Although written in 1860, this passage could probably describe many of the freestanding houses of generations of blacks in Richmond from the 1700s to emancipation:

> It was a hovel built...of brick-bats and mud, and as the ground on which it stood formed a trapezium, he adopted his edifice to it. Square and plumb had nothing to do with the lines of its walls. The materials were gathered from the ruins of old buildings, or the refuse of new ones, and as they were gathered, the structure progressed. The roof was of boards, or slates or slabs, which ever came to hand, and the chimneys were topped with headless barrels. [15]

The location of Hawkins's house, situated on an oddly shaped plot of wasteland on Brook Turnpike, may be typical of houses of African Americans who of necessity were forced to build on land deemed otherwise unsuitable and worthless. Often these houses clung to the steep terrain of Richmond's dramatic hillsides and bottoms, convenient to employment in the homes of whites located in healthier locations at the top of Richmond's hills, but still discreetly out of sight. Richmond's African Americans were often shoehorned into bottoms or in the labyrinths of named alleys that once complicated the Richmond street grid.

When Richmond became a city in 1782, the system of slavery was in full swing throughout the fledgling commonwealth, with businesses, industries and countless private households relying on the system of bondage for their day-to-day operations and success. Sometimes slaves belonged to the owners of the businesses, but often they were slaves who had been "hired out," a system that was common throughout the entire slavery era. The practice of hiring out was simple enough: a slave owner would negotiate with someone who needed temporary or seasonal labor. In such cases the owners would essentially rent out their slaves for an agreed-upon price, with the slaves' owners receiving the money. On other occasions, owners would allow their slaves to seek their own employment and find their own lodging, the stipulation being that the slaves would have to relinquish their salaries to their owners. Free African Americans supplemented slave labor by negotiating their own employment contracts according to their skills and abilities.

The ruins of one of the factories that employed thousands of black manual laborers, skilled freemen and white workmen over the years still stand in Richmond as a monument to their industry. The remains of the Tredegar Iron Works can still be seen along the banks of the James in present-day Richmond. The facilities of the Tredegar Iron Works consisted of five acres of buildings. These included furnaces, mills, warehouses, a separate three-story spike factory, foundry, machine shop and locomotive works. All were located along the river and canal below Gamble's Hill.

Squalid housing, such as that shown here in Shockoe Valley, constituted the living quarters for many of Richmond's blacks and poor whites in the nineteenth century. *Courtesy City of Richmond, Mayor's Annual Report to City Council for 1914.*

This nineteenth-century image depicts Tredegar Iron Works in full operation. Known as the "Ironmaker of the Confederacy," it depended largely upon slave labor. *Courtesy Library of Virginia.*

The boiler shop at Tredegar was housed in a building 160 feet long, and these and the other workshops were among the largest structures in Richmond.[16] Slaves were also housed on the Tredegar property following a bitter strike by white workers in 1847, probably in four multi-unit tenements that were located on the grounds.[17] For many African Americans of the period, the only world they knew was in the shadow of the belching smokestacks of the Tredegar furnaces. By the eve of the Civil War, Tredegar employed more than a hundred slaves and free blacks.[18] The complex of buildings that provided food, housing and support for this workforce was the pride of the city and would have been cited as proof of Richmond's importance in antebellum America.

Although horrific to modern sensibilities, another source of civic pride was the scale of slave labor in Richmond. The extent and influence of this human-powered industry were staggering, and its effect on the built environment of the city was considerable. "What made Richmond's economic prosperity most impressive, however—and unique in the antebellum South—was the thousands of slave laborers who pulled and pressed the tobacco, forged the iron, and ground the wheat," noted a recent history of slavery in the city.[19]

Today, the view from Gamble's Hill above the remains of Tredegar is of a pleasant river valley with the James moving languidly over the falls and the sound of the water interrupted only by traffic or a passing coal train. Two hundred years ago, however, this area and many other industrial sites all over the city were continually busy producing machinery and cannons or grinding grains and coffee. Canal boat traffic from the west and seagoing vessels in the eastern end of the riverfront moved raw materials into the city and moved finished products out of the city.

Little remains today of the famous Tredegar Iron Works, once one of Richmond's premier industries that employed free blacks and slaves alike. Its ruins, shown here, serve as a visitors' center.

BUILT BY BLACKS

Throughout, black hands wielded the tools, moved the cargo and managed the transport that made antebellum Richmond hum. They built the houses and sheds, the wharves and warehouses and the roads and bridges that made it all possible. The commercial promise of the falls of the James was realized with black labor driving the transformation from scenic river valley to industrial dynamo. From the earliest days of the city until emancipation, black laborers, to a large extent, laid the brick and granite foundation of the Richmond we know today.

2

The Slave Markets
in Shockoe Valley

"I could hear them mournin' and prayin'."
—A slave auction witness

The modern traveler approaches Richmond from the south on Interstate 95, a six-lane ribbon of highway that flows through the city carrying a current of cars and trucks. The highway leaps across the James River east of downtown and, still elevated several stories in the air, passes over the valley of Shockoe Creek. Travelers look down from this height onto an unremarkable collection of rooftops and parking lots, with only the glimpse of a dormer window or old brick chimney to hint at the antiquity of the neighborhoods below.

Passing the clay-tiled roof and clock tower of Main Street Station, the highway is anchored on an earth embankment. Glancing to the east from the northbound lanes, there is a view lasting only a few seconds of railroad tracks, warehouses, parking lots and the green of Church Hill rising up on the other side of the valley. Travelers have only seconds to glance across the valley before they are swept along by traffic. Yet in that brief time, their vision has taken in what 150 years ago was the dark heart of the slave trade in America. Even from the valley floor, below the interstate, there is little to hint of this past, but the bleak story of this part of Richmond and this period of American history is slowly being brought to light.

In 2006, the Alliance to Conserve Old Richmond Neighborhoods (ACORN), the Virginia Department of Historic Resources, the City of Richmond and the Richmond Slave Trail Commission cosponsored an archaeological survey on the site of Lumpkin's Jail, the most infamous of the slave-trading facilities that lined the streets and alleys of Shockoe Valley.[1] Although termed a "jail," this half-acre compound owned by Robert Lumpkin was much more than a pen for the enslaved.

It was the epitome of a commodious and efficient mid-nineteenth-century Richmond business complex. It included the owner's house, a guest house for out-of-town customers and substantial dining facilities, including a barroom. Standing within the same walled compound as these inviting surroundings, however, were more sinister accommodations. For it was here that, during the pre–Civil War years, Lumpkin also housed the thousands of slaves he bartered throughout the South, until the collapse of the Confederacy put an end to his business.

While Lumpkin's customers were enjoying his hospitality, the unfortunate chattel housed elsewhere in his compound experienced the most degrading of all the horrors of the slave trade. They were there to be sold—children being torn from mothers, wives from husbands, friends from friends and brothers from sisters.

The masses of African Americans who passed through the gates of Richmond businesses such as Lumpkin's Jail left few records of their experiences. The vast majority was not literate. Those who were may have been reluctant to revisit such memories. However, some ex-slaves did and their voices have to speak for the thousands who suffered and departed into history in silence. Even a brief description of the slave trade and how it was conducted is enough to evoke the sounds and sights that once filled the now comparatively bland streets and alleys of Shockoe Valley:

> *The speculators stayed in the hotel and put the niggers in the quarters jes like droves of hogs. All through the night I could hear them mournin' and prayin.' I didn't know the Lord would let people live who were so cruel. The gates were always locked and they was a guard on the outside to shoot anyone who tried to run away. Lord miss, them slaves look jes like droves of turkeys runnin' along in front of them horses. I remember when they put 'em on the block to sell 'em. The ones 'tween 18 and 30 always bring the most money. The auctioneer he stand off at a distances and cry 'em off as they stand on the block. I can hear his voice as long as I live.*[2]

For generations, the sights described in this passage were common in slave markets of the city. Thousands of African Americans passed through the streets of Richmond as they made

Above left and right: Henry Brown, a slave owned by William Barret, gained international fame when he had an accomplice ship him to Philadelphia in a box measuring two by three feet. Brown, whose journey earned him the nickname "Box," undertook the desperate venture following the sale of his wife and children by a Richmond slave dealer. Pictured at right is Brown's house, at 15 South Fifth Street.

their way to the auction houses, looking up apprehensively at the towering hotels, grand homes, tall mills and smoking chimneys of the antebellum industrial metropolis. These structures loomed over them like canyons of red brick, impressive in their scale and often oppressive in their purpose.

For newly arrived slaves, Richmond must have been a place of astonishing dread; a vision of hell for which no folk tale could have prepared them. For the slave being trans-shipped to the American interior, Richmond must have seemed like a plantation writ large: impossibly industrious and grimly purposeful. Richmond's reputation as a slave center is well dramatized in Henry "Box" Brown's work, *Narrative of the Life of Henry "Box" Brown* (1851).

Separated from his wife, Brown knew the indignities of Richmond's slave jails. So horrified was he by his experience of slavery that he escaped from Richmond nailed in a box, an act that gained him international fame. Similarly, national outrage was stirred by the experiences of fugitive slave Anthony Burns, who was captured in the North and imprisoned at Lumpkin's Jail.

A preliminary archaeological survey at the Lumpkin's Jail site in 2006 produced nearly a thousand artifacts as well as sections of a foundation.

Artifacts unearthed in the summer of 2006 at the site of Robert Lumpkin's slave business, locally called "the Devil's half acre."

The African Americans, whose path took them through the city streets, represented a commodity much like wheat, coffee or tobacco; they flowed through Richmond in wagons, on ships and in canal boats. The newly arrived slaves may have peered fearfully into the eyes of the whites who regarded them along the raised wooden sidewalks, perhaps in the same vicinity that Booker T. Washington had spent the night sleeping under one.[3] Their cool expressions of appraisal were like those of a buyer in the marketplace, or of a manufacturer assessing new machinery. Fellow African Americans may have regarded them with a mixture of sympathy and scorn: sympathy for their plight and scorn for their ignorance when entering the ways of the city's slave world. The bustle of Richmond's business district along Main Street, the streets teeming with whites and blacks going about their tasks, must have seemed for rural slaves like a kaleidoscope of people and buildings.

If scenes such as these took place in the winter it was all the more frightening, especially for slaves being herded to and from the auction houses.

> *The ebb and flow of the* [slave] *hiring system peaked during the Christmas season when thousands of African Americans returned to friends and family in the country for the holidays, returning for the hiring season after the new year.*[4]

As a center of slave trade, Richmond drew surplus slaves from the surrounding countryside. When they were not needed on the farms, these slaves would be hired out to Richmond industries. Thus the streets of the city were alive with humanity, much of it composed of peripatetic African Americans searching for work during the coming year. Buffeted by all these sensations and sights, unfamiliar smells and sounds, the path of the slave wound inexorably downhill toward Shockoe Valley.

Today, much of the Richmond that the enslaved and free African Americans of the antebellum period knew has changed, and many of the steep hills and dramatic gullies that once defined the topography of the city have been reduced and filled. The looming buildings of the nineteenth century have been replaced with modern towers ten times as tall.

Nevertheless, modern Richmonders live on the same grid of streets that the enslaved African Americans walked, and the earth below modern Richmond holds many secrets from slavery days. As the Lumpkin's Jail archaeological survey has indicated, artifacts, lost graves, hidden streams and the buried foundations of once well-known buildings that were landmarks in their day still lurk below streets and sidewalks to tell their tales. In the valley, Shockoe Creek was, and remains, an irresistible force of water that drains a large portion of Richmond, extending some miles to the north. Early attempts to first channel the stream and bridge it for the streets that ran east and west were expensive and often futile due to the floods and freshets that would back up from the James River and reclaim Shockoe Valley. Shockoe Creek was eventually forced into a giant culvert, where unseen and unheard, its underground waters still seek the James River.

The story of the slave industry in Shockoe is much like that of the creek of the same name. From the valley floor, there is nothing to suggest anything sinister about the Shockoe

Valley landscape, with Main Street Station and the interstate highway dominating the vista. A section of the area is given over to restored Victorian buildings containing restaurants and some small industries. Other blocks have been cleared of buildings and now serve as surface parking for legions of state employees who toil up Broad Street hill to their jobs.

In many of these demolished blocks, a delicate skein of alleys can still be seen where over fifty slave traders once operated. These cobblestone survivors remain to locate the old blocks and intersections of vanished streets. The simple crossing of these cobblestone lines often delineates the area of Richmond's slave-trading industry, where it once stood in Shockoe Valley, and the territory of all the misery, pain and anguish. Two extant buildings are associated with the slave trade in Richmond: one an auction house at 1423 East Cary Street and the other a commission merchant's building at 15 South Fifteenth Street. It is good that emotion does not leave its imprint on its surroundings, for this area of the city would be forever stained deep into the earth by the gallons of tears shed within the precincts of several city blocks of antebellum Richmond. If the cries of those being "sold down the river," or "sold south," and those who were left behind entered the ground, there would be a reservoir of shrieks and moans below the cobblestones that time could never silence.

Beaver,
" Nutrie,
" Moleskin,
" Silk,

All or any of which will be sold on accommodating terms.
JOHN THOMPSON & CO.
June 9   9—2aw4w

NOTICE.—ONE HUNDRED NEGROES WANTED—The subscriber will pay the highest cash prices for one hundred likely young Negroes, consisting of males and females, from 12 to 25 years of age. Sempstresses and mechanics, of all descriptions, will also be purchased at liberal prices. I can be found at all times at my office, adjoining my private jail, not more than 150 yards in the rear of the Bell Tavern in the City of Richmond. All persons coming to the city with slaves for sale, are requested to give me a call before they sell their property, by so doing, they can at all times obtain the highest market price.
N. MATTHEWS
Richmond, Va. June 13, 1843.   10—8t

LOST.—The person or persons who have the Files of the Enquirer for the years from 9th May, 1807, to 9th May, 1808; from 9th May, 1811, to 9th May, 1812; from 9th May, 1813, to 9th May, 1814; from 9th May, 1817, to 9th May, 1818; and from 9th May, 1818, to 9th May, 1819, belonging to the Enquirer Office, are

Notices such as these were regularly published in Richmond's newspapers during the height of the city's slavery era. *Courtesy Library of Virginia.*

On the eve of the Civil War, Richmond was the leading export center for slaves to the Deep South. This engraving, from the *London Illustrator*, 1861, depicts a slave auction in Shockoe Valley, where the trade was centered. *Courtesy Valentine Richmond History Center.*

The essential and defining act of American slavery was the slave auction, and it was here in Shockoe Valley where the slave auction houses were located.

> *Nothing symbolizes the fragility and inequities of slave life better than the slave auction. Hundreds of thousands of slaves throughout the South experienced the uncertainty, the humiliation, the fear, and the psychological shock that accompanied the domestic slave trade.*[5]

The mechanics of the slave auction and the threat of separation from family and home were bitterly traumatic and the malaise permeated Shockoe Valley. The slave's world could change in an instant based on the whims of the owner. Slaves were sold for almost any reason, from the need for money to the need to settle an estate or an owner's displeasure with a particular slave. In fact, the threat of selling a slave became one of an owner's weapons to enforce discipline and exercise control. The threat of transportation to Richmond meant only one thing. News that a relative or spouse was bound for the city could signal the end of a marriage, the division of a family or a future of extreme hardship in the Deep South, where the weather was hotter and the backbreaking workday longer.

Given Richmond's mid-Atlantic location and its number of railroad lines, roads and waterways, it became a leading export center for all commerce, including slaves. The buildings of Shockoe Valley were the stages upon which this process was enacted. The names of the businesses could be those of any commission merchant, dry goods dealer or commodity broker, but in antebellum Richmond these innocuous labels struck dread into the hearts of African Americans. For many, it was the first experience of the built environment of Richmond. For thousands, these buildings were the scene of their meager lives coming undone. The auction houses and slave jails became an attraction for visitors to Richmond much in the same way that tourists visit factories today. Writers from places other than the American South would describe these trading facilities in terms of "broken families, of humans treated less with cruelty than like so many head of valuable livestock."[6] Dozens of full- and part-time traders in other commodities also sold African Americans to buyers from across the Southern United States.

Strong black field hands and mulatto house servants were sold to Deep South buyers by Ben Davis, Dickenson & Hill, Pulliam & Betts, Browning & Moore, Silas Omohundro, McDaniel & Blackburn, Robert Lumpkin, and others.[7]

With the depletion of Virginia's soil under the burden of overcultivation of tobacco and cotton, her planters began to sell their surplus property in the form of African Americans on the Richmond market. New Orleans was the only American city whose trade in enslaved blacks exceeded Richmond. But it was Richmond that was the leader in the export business, and by 1860 this amounted to more than $4 million a year.[8] In the decades just prior to the Civil War, Richmond replaced cities like Alexandria as the center of trade for the upper South, and the low, mean warehouses of Shockoe Valley were central to the trade.

The area where this trade took place was concentrated in a part of the city less than a ten-minute walk from the State Capitol building on Shockoe Hill, an icon of American democracy that was largely built with slave labor. Geographically, the slave-trading area centered on the Bell Tavern (later known as the City Hotel) at Main and Fifteenth Streets. From this point it was a short walk up Fifteenth Street to find the small alleys and muddy streets in the shadow of the steep valley wall. A safe distance from the stench of the slave jails, fashionable hotels such as the Exchange and the St. Charles were important sites for the slave trade. These places often housed the offices of slave dealers, where buyers could be received in relative comfort and style. The hotels also afforded accommodations for buyers of African Americans who had made the long trip from Danville, Raleigh or points farther south to come to this vast mart to buy. The basement of the Odd Fellows Hall at Franklin and Fourteenth Streets was the scene of many such auctions. Above the streets of Shockoe Valley, the appearance of a red flag signaled to interested buyers that an auction was to take place at that particular site. Buyers must have glimpsed that scarlet banner in the distance and hustled toward it through the muddy streets, eager to trade and anxious not to miss out on a "likely" African American.[9]

The St. Charles Hotel, located at Fifteenth and Main Streets, was one of the city's premier hotels prior to the Civil War. Slaves were auctioned on the premises in rooms on the first floor. *Courtesy Valentine Richmond History Center.*

A list of slave dealers and their addresses compiled in 1993 gives an idea of the magnitude of the slave trade in Shockoe Valley between 1840 and 1860. Along Franklin Street, at the Bell Tavern on Main Street and tucked into Birch Alley, Locust Alley, Exchange Alley and Wall Street (now Fifteenth Street) were over fifty slave-trading facilities.

Five slave jails were concentrated along Birch Alley, which was also known as Lumpkin's Alley, named after Robert Lumpkin's establishment.[10] This conglomeration of slave-trading facilities, jammed together with their barred windows, high fences and chained gates opening onto the rutted streets, and all seen and smelled through a film of cooking smoke and the stench of human excrement, must have made a dreadful landscape.

Above it all was the red banner signaling the end of another black family or the forcible transportation of an African American from a Richmond slave auction house.

A number of descriptions, some fanciful and some factual, of the slave jails exist. Recently, when a former slave jail was discovered in Kentucky, an African American trustee emeritus of the National Trust for Preservation noted, "It's nothing but a pile of logs. Yet it is everything. It was a slave ship turned upside down."[11]

Richmond slave dealer Hector Davis was the proprietor of just such a place, long since demolished but which nevertheless lives on in the description of a woman who visited the facility when it was still standing in the mid-twentieth century. While in business, Davis had described himself as "Auctioneer and Commission Merchant for Sale of Negroes," and his establishment was on East Franklin Street between the Ballard Hotel and Fifteenth Street, in the heart of Shockoe Valley. Davis pledged his best efforts to obtain the highest market prices. "He [Davis wrote of himself in the third person] has a safe and commodious jail where he will board all negroes intended for his sale at 30 cents per day."[12] Davis's dungeon-like slave facility, still standing in 1937, was described in a report as a brick and stone structure of "strongly restraining"[13] materials.

Betts & Gregory,
AUCTIONEERS,
Franklin Street,
RICHMOND, VA.

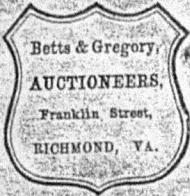

Richmond, *August 7 1860.*

Dear Sir:

We beg leave to give you the state of our Negro Market, and quote them as follows:

Extra Men,	$ 1550	to $ 1625
No. 1 do.	$ 1450	to $ 1550
Second rate or Ordinary do.	$ 1100	to $ 1250
Extra Girls,	$ 1375	to $ 1450
No. 1 do.	$ 1300	to $ 1350
Second rate or Ordinary do.	$ 900	to $ 1100
Boys 4 feet high,	$ 500	to $ 600
Boys 4 feet 3 inches high,	$ 600	to $ 700
Boys 4 feet 6 inches high,	$ 800	to $ 900
Boys 4 feet 9 inches high,	$ 1000	to $ 1100
Boys 5 feet high,	$ 1100	to $ 1250

Girls of same height of boys about the same prices.

Good young woman & first child $1300 to $1450

The Market is dull this week owing to the fact that there are but few Southern buyers in the market. — We do not

Yours Respy,
Betts & Gregory

Chapin Library Williams College

This 1860 price list offers a glimpse into the economics of the "Negro Market" in Richmond. The auction company, Betts & Gregory, located in Shockoe Valley, offered blacks for sale on an escalating price scale: the taller the person, the higher the sale price. *Courtesy Library of Virginia.*

A narrow entry off Fifteenth Street, just wide enough to accommodate a wagon, opened into Davis's courtyard. There, in the center of this pit of misery, a small shed enclosure was the scene of the auction of humans and livestock alike. A particularly poignant description of the jail can be found in the testimony of a former Confederate general, who visited the auction house with Daisy Avery, author of the 1937 report.

General William M. Evans, then ninety years old, accompanied the writer to the location and stated that his own father took him there years before and had purchased his "black mammy"—pointing out an approximate place where she was sitting when they arrived.[14]

Avery, who wrote the 1937 description of the building, evidently felt the palpable dread of Hector Davis's auction house. The exact location of Davis's establishment, hard against the hillside of what is now downtown Richmond, is evident from her description:

The ground floor has heavy restraining walls against the sheer hillside on the west side of the building. The north wall is of huge stone blocks, and at the eastern end of the north wall is an archway built of stone, and now bricked in with bricks that are thickly covered with old moss. This archway gave upon a rear alley of only a few feet, due to the hillside that must have been cut away for the north wall. A stream of water flowed from a spring in the hillside, and evidence of this is still visible. There is just enough room for a wagon to have driven in from Wall Street [now Fifteenth] and entered the "compound." The auction bell tower is still discernible, although it has been cut down and the bell long removed…In the center of the Court stands a rickety shed-like structure, topped in the center with a large tower, and a smaller one to the north; this shed was used for sales of both humans and livestock.[15]

The site of Hector Davis's livestock and human sales facility is probably buried deep beneath Interstate 95, just down the hill from the Virginia Commonwealth University Medical Center (formerly the Medical College of Virginia). Despite its having been demolished and covered by dirt and fill, its presence remains in history. The sweat-slick floors, the bloody doorsills and the unyielding damp stone still linger in memory and imagination. The irony of the location of slave jails like Hector Davis's was not lost on Avery. Under the heading "Historical Significance" on the form used to describe the building, she noted the geographic location of the slave trade to "civilized" Richmond.

Attention is called to the proximity of the most fashionable hotels, the Exchange and Ballard, also the churches and theaters, on the south side of the same street, within two or three blocks distance.[16]

Again and again commentators on the slave trade in Richmond make the point of the inherent proximity of this traffic in humans to the daily life of Richmond.

Writing in 1899, John S. Wise recalled being invited to visit a slave sale:

> Out of the beautiful gardens and past the handsome residences we went, turning down
> Franklin Street towards the great Exchange Hotel, which at that time was the principal public
> place of Richmond. Beyond it we passed a church, still used as such, although the locality had
> been deserted by residences, and stables and the little shops surrounded it. As we proceeded,
> the street became more and more squalid and repulsive, until at last we reached a low brick
> warehouse, with its end abutting the street and running far back. Over the place was a sign,
> with the name of an owner and the words "Auction House" conspicuously painted. At the
> door hung a red flag, with an advertisement pasted on its side, and up and down the street a
> mulatto man walked with another flag, ringing a large bell, shouting "Oh, yea! Oh yea! Walk
> up, gentlemen. The sale of a fine, likely lot of young niggers is about to begin."[17]

This trade was regarded as just another commercial enterprise in the heart of Richmond. It emphasizes the acceptance of slavery as a business and the buildings where it was conducted as a vital part of the fabric of the city. Richmonders of the day would have enumerated the slave industry as one of the economic resources of the city, much in the same way as the tall mills that dominated the riverfront.

Robert Lumpkin was an astute businessman whose wife Mary had formerly been one of his slaves. Such was the infamy connected with Lumpkin's walled compound that it became widely known, especially among the city's African Americans, as "the Devil's half-acre," a fitting term for a veritable factory of misery.[18]

Charles H. Corey described Lumpkin's slave market in 1895, and his impressions give a good idea of both the architecture of this much-feared establishment and its setting below Shockoe Hill:

Demolished in 1876, Robert Lumpkin's slave jail compound included lodging for slave traders, a slave-holding facility and auction house, as well as a residence for his own family. Shown at right is the jail. Mary F. Lumpkin, Robert's African American widow, aided post–Civil War black education efforts when in 1867 she rented the jail complex to a school that evolved into Virginia Union University. *Courtesy Valentine Richmond History Center.*

> *Lumpkin's slave jail consisted of about half an acre of land near the center of the older portion of Richmond. The patch lay very low in a deep hollow or "bottom," as it might be called, through which a small stream of water ran very slowly. In reaching this place of sighs from Broad Street, one had to climb down the incline of a sandy embankment nearly one hundred feet. The descent was steep, irregular, and in places difficult. In approaching the place from the Franklin Street side, the descent was quite gradual and easy by means of a narrow, crooked, untidy lane. Around the outer borders of the said half-acre was a fence, in some places ten or twelve feet in height. Inside of the fence, and very close to it, was a tall old brick building, which Lumpkin had used for his dwelling-house. Near by were other buildings, also of brick, where he used to shelter the more peaceable of his slave-gangs that were brought to him from time to time to be sold. But in the corner of the plot was the chief object of interest—a low, rough, brick building known as the "slave jail." In this building Lumpkin was accustomed to imprison the disobedient and punish the refractory. The stout iron bars were still to be seen across one or more of the windows during my repeated visits to this place. In the rough floor, and about at the center of it, was the stout iron staple and whipping ring.*[19]

In the same volume, the functions of the buildings that made up the "Devil's half-acre" were described in detail:

> *One was used by the proprietor as his residence and his office. Another was used as a boarding-house for the accommodation of those who came to sell their slaves or buy. A third served as a bar-room and a kitchen. The "old jail" stood in a field a few rods from the other buildings. It was forty-one feet long and two stories in height, with a piazza to both stories on the north side of the building.*[20]

For historians, Lumpkin's Jail and its complex of support buildings have come to epitomize the Richmond slave market. This is largely because of these descriptions of its appearance and function. Images of the architecture of the slavery trade are rare, but Corey's *History of the Richmond Theological Seminary* also reproduces an illustration of the two-story jail. This picture, although somewhat crude, provides a glimpse into the center of one of the most notorious structures of the American slave trade.

The story of the building that was Lumpkin's Jail might be expected to end with the fall of Richmond in 1865 and the freeing of the slaves. Most of the structures of the slave trade in Shockoe Valley were either replaced with light industry during Reconstruction or they remained simply as warehouses until their eventual demolition.

In contrast, Lumpkin's Jail survived the war for years afterward and played a remarkable role in the education of former slaves and their descendants. According to Dr. Raymond Hylton, a Virginia Union University (VUU) professor of history, Dr. Nathan Colver was an elderly, hard-bitten abolitionist who had difficulty finding someone who would rent or sell property to house the school for blacks he was attempting to establish in postwar Richmond. Colver was close to despair when he had a chance encounter with Lumpkin's wife Mary, who rented him the former Lumpkin's Jail.[21]

Known as the Burial Ground for Negroes, this parking lot at Fifteenth and Broad Streets is the final resting place of countless Richmond blacks, both slave and free. Gabriel, the leader of an 1800 slave revolt, was executed on the nearby city gallows and in all likelihood is buried here.

As Colver described it, the slave pen was no longer "Devil's half-acre, but God's half acre."[22] This improbable turn of events was accepted to the point where the facility was now known matter-of-factly as Lumpkin's Jail School.[23] The architecture of despair had been turned into the architecture of hope and promise. The school moved to the former United States Hotel nearby on Main Street in 1870. Although it operated under several names in later years, this educational facility is the direct ancestor of VUU, which prides itself on rising from its ironic roots.

The preliminary archaeological survey at the site of Lumpkin's Jail in 2006 has only scratched the surface of the record below the ground of Shockoe Valley. The innocuous holes dug beside Interstate 95 hold the potential for changing the face of Richmond history and the record of antebellum America.[24]

As late as 1950, much of the architectural fabric of the Shockoe Valley where Richmond began was still intact. That year, Mary Wingfield Scott, one of the twentieth century's preeminent historians of the city, commented that the Shockoe Valley area, although decrepit, was still "one of the most interesting sections of Richmond, and at the same time one of its most woe-begone, whether from the material or human point of view."[25] The advent of the Richmond–Petersburg Turnpike in the late 1950s, however, buried much of the critically important area of Fifteenth Street under its grading along the east side of Shockoe Hill, and entire city blocks of buildings are now many feet under fill. Many city blocks south of Broad Street have been lost, as has the area surrounding Main Street Station, whose railroad tracks run across the site of so many buildings associated with the slave trade.

Another location critical to understanding the slave trade in Richmond still exists, albeit in a much disguised form. For the sick slave, one wounded by mistreatment or the victim of one of the "fevers" that sometimes swept through the slave jails in the valley, one last indignity remained. It was an anonymous grave in Richmond's slave burying ground north of Broad Street and on the west side of Shockoe Creek. Here, at the lowest part of the city, beside the fetid waters of Shockoe Creek, were the town gallows and cemetery for African Americans who died in bondage. It was in this dreaded place

The Davenport and Allen auction company occupied this building at Fifteenth and Cary Streets prior to the Civil War. It possibly is one of the few remaining city buildings from which slaves were sold in quantity.

that Gabriel, the leader of the slave rebellion of 1800, was executed and presumably buried with countless other slaves.[26]

Today, the slave burying ground, or the "Burial Ground for Negroes," as it was called, is all but forgotten and its past has been largely obscured by a succession of owners who neither knew nor cared about its original purpose. Covered by fill and debris and paved over, the site at 1550 East Broad Street is today a parking lot used by state employees. Yet for all the indignities that have been visited upon this spot, beneath the asphalt and beside the underground culvert that now contains Shockoe Creek, lie the bodies of an unknown number of African Americans. Their lives were hard and their fates not kind, but it was with their backs and by their hands that much of the antebellum city was built. Their last resting place is one of the least known and most abused and neglected African American historical sites in the city, perhaps in the nation. One can only hope that with a greater appreciation of the importance of the slave trade and Shockoe Valley, the slave burial ground will receive the attention and respect that it deserves.[27]

The story of the slave trade and the buildings associated with it is not popular. The architecture of the trade reverted back to industrial uses in Shockoe Valley after the Civil War and the low brick buildings that were once warehouses of humans turned to storehouses of railway supplies and farm machinery. Much of the fabric of the area was lost over the years to demolition and floods. Until the construction of the Richmond floodwall in the 1980s, the James River continued to back up into Shockoe Valley and lower Main Street as it had for millennia.

Current construction in what is becoming an increasingly popular area for residential and restaurant development occasionally reveals a sturdy brick foundation, a massive granite threshold or a heavy iron bracket. We would do well to remember the thousands who passed through the streets and the alleys, the markets and the jails and those whose callused hands brushed the unyielding walls. Those thousands of African Americans found shelter from only the weather in the buildings of Shockoe Valley. It would take a civil war to provide the shelter of law necessary to live as free citizens.

3

Urban Plantations
and the Civil War

"The houses of the wealthy perched on the hilltops."
—Nelson Lankford

The place where the separate worlds of free black, enslaved black and white antebellum Richmond most closely abutted was in the setting of domestic slavery. It was in the context of domestic service that whites sometimes welcomed and sometimes tolerated the presence of African Americans in their homes. It was here, in what one historian estimates was 50 percent of Richmond households, that slaves and free blacks entered the world of white Richmonders, cleaning their kitchens, preparing their meals, nursing the sick and the young and observing the world of whites from within.[1] The number of blacks serving in those homes was considerable. For example, one group of fifteen homes on Franklin Street employed almost a hundred slaves, a large population of blacks all operating behind doors and below stairs in this ostensibly white upper-class neighborhood.[2]

The boundaries between the worlds of master and slave were most plastic in the homes of white Richmonders where blacks served as domestic servants. Blurred by the lens of an idealized past, the perceived relationship was one of "family." Despite the various readings of this arrangement, from employment and opportunity to confinement in nothing more than a genteel jail, the high-style architecture of Richmond's grandest antebellum homes was for many blacks their first experience with the built environment of any architectural consequence or scale.

What most African Americans felt about the interaction inside the homes of whites has largely gone unrecorded. Certainly the life of a servant in the city version of the plantation "Big House" was, at first examination, a superior existence free from the harsh labor in the field and the stereotypically sadistic overseer. On the other hand, it has been noted that the domestic slave did not find protection in the large numbers and anonymity of an expansive operation. Unlike the work of artisans, drivers or watermen, slaves' performances in domestic service in the city were subject to unrelenting examination and criticism.[3] The "Big House," be it a plantation mansion or the urban villa of a wealthy white Richmonder, was an arena where working with and among whites brought extraordinary privileges but also extraordinary pressures. The confident and articulate exterior of an African American in service in a white Richmond household could still conceal pain and distress. Fine clothes and high station were not always a godsend. Nor did a grand house necessarily imply protection from the same abuse that might occur on a backwoods farm.[4]

What remains from antebellum Richmond to testify to the complex life of urban slavery and servitude are the grand homes of the city's early neighborhoods. This is ironic, for the lifestyle of the wealthy and elite was far from the experiences of enslaved or even free blacks in Richmond, and so little survives to document the domestic life of African Americans in the city. With the loss of much of Richmond's architectural heritage of all kinds through the years (and particularly among those vernacular homes of common citizens, black and white), we often have to satisfy ourselves with an examination of this facet of Richmond's African American history as seen in surviving high-style homes.

The houses of white slave owners varied in size, number of blacks employed and the social status of the owner. They ranged from very modest homes where a slave would be hired as cook or nurse rather than owned outright, to grand residences where a slave spent a lifetime dedicated to a specific task. These larger homes were essentially plantations on a small scale, reproducing in miniature the mansion and supporting buildings seen in the Virginia countryside. Where work in the country was in agricultural production, the urban plantation was geared toward the function of the household.

Unlike the rural plantation, construction costs could be high and space was at a premium even in the largest houses in the city. Boardinghouses and tenements for African Americans became an element of the urban landscape in Richmond, with the relative freedom that these "homes" provided. These were made even more common by the practice of hiring out laborers, who also had to find accommodations within walking distance of their employers and whose allowance for board could be spent on whatever housing could be found. Those who had to stay on the premises might find a spot to sleep in a barn, stable or simply by rolling up their bedding in a room used during the day.[5] Writing in his *American City, Southern Place: A Cultural History of Antebellum Richmond*, Gregg D. Kimball notes that housing on the grounds of Richmond's upper-class homes was often reserved for African American women, while black men typically found lodgings throughout the city wherever they could.

Richmond's prosperous neighborhoods—Church Hill below Broad Street, Shockoe Hill and West Franklin and Grace Streets—presented an impressive façade of Federal and Greek revival townhouses. A cluster of outbuildings supported each household. Slaves in domestic service typically lived in two-story dwellings amid smokehouses, necessaries, carriage houses and other dependencies. The first floor of the quarters often housed the laundry and main kitchen, thus removing a fire hazard and unpleasant smells from the main house.[6]

The most grand and lavish of Richmond's mansions tended to be located on the hills above the city. "The houses of the wealthy perched on the hilltops, architectural testimony that white Richmond constituted one of the most prosperous communities in America."[7] Many of the lavish homes looked down from the heights directly into Shockoe Valley and the industry of slavery. It was on the very brink of the valley that a Richmond banker named Brockenbrough built in 1818 the fashionable mansion at 1201 East Clay Street that later became the home of Confederate President Jefferson Davis and his family. The gardens of the White House of the Confederacy spilled down the hillside, with inviting vistas of the Shockoe Valley and all that it contained. From the bottom of their garden the Brockenbroughs and their successors, the Davis family, could easily see the roofs of the slave jails from the steep hillside below their house.[8]

The relationship between the buildings and homes of slave-owning whites, the blacks who worked in these homes, their own houses or tenements and Shockoe Valley is critical in understanding the built environment of antebellum Richmond. This vista of the slave markets was for blacks a reminder of not only affronts of the past, but worse, the constant threat of being sold "down the river" should they not perform to their masters' requirements. A red flag flown at the slave auction houses was highly visible to most of the city, as it was intended. This blood-red banner could be seen from the kitchen yard of a grand home, from the shacks of the upper Shockoe Valley, from the great mills along the river and from the canal. The mansion on the hill, the urban quarters and the factories of the city were the manifestations of a society knit together with sinews of iron chain. These lines all crossed in Shockoe Valley, and everyone in Richmond, white and black, free and slave, was aware of the confluence. This societal and architectural fault line would ultimately collapse and with it the world of antebellum Richmond.

Good examples of the high-style pre–Civil War homes remain in Richmond. Many have in the intervening years lost much of the context that included the auxiliary buildings where their slave staff worked and lived. Those constructed of brick and in proximity to the main house often survive. This tends to be more common in areas such as Church Hill, where the small lots dictated close grouping of the main structure and the often detached kitchen. A good example is the Hilary Baker house at 2302 East Grace Street, whose original structure dates to 1813. The two-story quarters behind the house is typical of the type that once was commonly found in the alleys of Church Hill.[9]

Another excellent example of the urban villa in a compact setting is the Hargrove house, located at 2300 East Grace Street next to the Hilary Baker house. Built in 1849, this large townhouse is a good example of the Greek revival style so popular in antebellum Richmond. Behind the house, hidden by a tall brick wall that shelters the business of the household from the street, two dependencies still stand. A four-bay, two-story building with porches facing the yard was a kitchen and slave quarters that are among the best surviving examples in the city.[10] Today the smaller of the two outbuildings serves as storage, but for many years it housed a business that supported the Hargrove family. Tobacco factory owner Thomas Hargrove built the house and the smaller one-story dependency, which would be the site of Hargrove's experiments in processing tobacco. Among the slaves in Hargrove's employ who worked in his tobacco factory and who certainly knew the Hargrove house yard well was John Jasper. Jasper underwent a religious conversion while stemming tobacco and, armed with this faith, eventually went on to found Sixth Mt. Zion Baptist Church.[11]

This relationship between the founder of one of Richmond's largest and most important African American churches and the Hargrove house on Church Hill draws one of many direct lines from the antebellum to the emancipated city. It underscores the connectivity between these culturally and architecturally dissimilar structures and neighborhoods, a tie that is hardly apparent today. The progression from the Hargrove house yard to today's Sixth Mt. Zion Baptist Church is a remarkable story, one of many in the history of African Americans in Richmond in which events in humble structures lead to ultimately sophisticated architectural achievement.

Other examples of outbuildings that formed part of the "urban plantation" infrastructure can be found behind various antebellum houses on Church Hill. The last grand mansion constructed in Richmond before the Civil War may also be termed the site of the last large urban slave quarters constructed before emancipation. The Pace-King House, below Church Hill at 205 North Nineteenth Street, was constructed in 1860. Its builder, Charles Hill, is described as an "auctioneer and local politician,"[12] and he may very well have played a role in the slave trade, which was located only blocks from his home.[13] In the yard is a two-story quarters in the usual pattern of having a gallery down one side to service and shelter entrances into the yard. The long side of the outbuilding also served to provide privacy for the rear yard of the house. The location of such a very stylish home, with its lavish cast-iron decoration, is unusual in Shockoe Valley. Here the slave markets would have been only just out of sight, a few blocks away across the sloping floor of Shockoe Valley.

Nearby, at 1812 East Grace, stands the Adam Craig house whose one dependency remains from what had been several antebellum buildings.[14] The brick kitchen at the rear of this house is a good example of a utilitarian outbuilding of the type that African Americans would have often worked and lived in, a functional structure without the architectural sophistication of the later buildings found behind the Pace-King House.

The Adam Craig house predates the grid of Richmond and was originally surrounded by an entire city block of property when constructed in 1784. Described as "rural-looking" even in 1860, this is a rare survivor of a building that made the transition from suburban plantation complex to being located today in the heart of the city.[15] The roles of the African Americans who must have lived and worked on the site no doubt changed over the years as the city grew up around the Adam Craig house and its property grew smaller. Several generations of blacks who served on this plot probably began their duties as small farmers for the needs of the household, growing vegetables and perhaps keeping cows in the fields around the house. As the city encroached, lots were sold off the property and urban conveniences at the nearby market became more sophisticated; thus the duties of the African Americans who labored at the Adam Craig house became more like those of their contemporaries on the small lots and grand houses of Church Hill.

Perhaps the largest and most coherent collection of slave quarters that served Richmond's grand Greek revival homes can still be found in what was then the western part of town behind Linden Row at 100–114 East Franklin Street. These row houses, built in 1847 and 1853, are the surviving eight of the original ten houses, each with its servants' quarters behind it. Today the rear yards have lost their functionality and have been made into decorative gardens to embellish hotel rooms located in the former row houses. Linden Row Inn now operates the entire complex as a hotel.

To service such a densely grouped population in these town houses, each with its own staff, needs, purchasing demands and demographics, there must have been an enormous amount of activity in the cobblestone alley behind the block-long row of houses. In the years before the Civil War, the alley behind Linden Row would have been busy as horses, wagons, slaves and free tradesmen of both colors attended to the needs of the families who lived there. Deliveries of coal, wood, food and laundry, and the foot traffic, would have been considerable.

Today the alley behind Linden Row is quiet and hints at none of the former bustle, with only an occasional car or truck to break the silence. Where the scent of wood smoke from cooking once competed with the smell of privies and horses, only crepe myrtles now move in the breeze. Nothing louder than the murmuring voices of tourists is heard in the Linden Row courtyards today, courtyards once filled with the sound of chopping wood, the creak of harnesses, the cluck of chickens and the voices of the African Americans who enabled the urban life in these row houses to function. Although the former life is gone from this small section of the city, the architecture remains for the imagination to repopulate the scene of this lost world of the antebellum "urban plantation."

The records of the Mutual Assurance Society of Virginia, which are part of the collection of the Library of Virginia, document the scope of outbuildings on the urban plantations of the city. Within their pages brief descriptions of outbuildings are often accompanied by sketches of the various quarters, stables, kitchens and offices that were the world of African Americans who served the city's "Big Houses." Hundreds of these outbuildings appear on the insurance policies, generally only as outlines on a plat. Although they were reduced to simple boxes under the pen of an insurance agent of the day, these outbuildings were the homes and workplaces of generations of enslaved African Americans in Richmond before the Civil War. The simple structures constituted the world

Built on the eve of the Civil War, the Pace-King House at 205 North Nineteenth Street is one of Richmond's last "urban plantations." Its slave quarters, shown here, were built to house a large staff.

of generations of black Richmonders who would instantly recognize each barn, stable, storehouse and kitchen and its occupant.[16]

As an example, the famous Union sympathizer Elizabeth Van Lew lived in an imposing mansion that stood on the south edge of Church Hill. The original house was constructed in 1802 and demolished in 1911. This is now the site of the present Bellevue School on the 2300 block of East Grace Street.[17] A Mutual Assurance Society policy for the Van Lew house shows a combination of servants' quarters and a kitchen building constructed of brick on the east side of the property.[18]

For Federal soldiers who escaped the various Confederate prisons in Richmond, the Van Lew Mansion "was the principal place of refuge for prisoners in the city." The very fabric of the house itself became part of the conspiracy to conceal escapees and shelter them from the vigilance of the authorities. In the attic was a secret room where fugitive Federals waited for an opportunity to flee the Confederate capital.[19]

The substantial quarters building is noteworthy on several levels. This building was probably the scene of many transfers of intelligence gleaned from the kitchens, stables and markets of Richmond and the surrounding rural area. This house was the center of a network of informants who kept Van Lew current on the activities of the Confederate government. Here, whispered accounts, rumors and observations gathered by hundreds

These slave quarters, built between 1847 and 1853 on the 100 block of East Franklin Street known as Linden Row, are typical of those located behind Richmond row houses in the antebellum period.

of spies around the Confederate capital would have probably been collected before passing on to Van Lew herself.[20] In appearance, the Van Lew quarters building was probably similar to, and a larger version of, the building still standing in the backyard of the nearby Hargrove house.

In addition to its importance to Confederate history, the Van Lew Mansion was also an African American landmark. It was the childhood home of Maggie Walker, a prominent black banker and entrepreneur who is covered more fully later in this book.

Walker's childhood in Richmond would have been filled with relatives who had worked on the urban plantations during the slavery era, and this memory may have contributed to her determination to lead and achieve in later life.[21] Again, subtle links are seen that stretch across the city of Richmond between cultures and neighborhoods, links that weave together the history of the city's people, black and white. Here, the setting of one of the most architecturally dramatic homes built by the slaveholding elite is the backdrop for events critical to African American history in the city. The culture of slavery sheltered the driving force that so influenced the built environment during the golden age of Jackson Ward.

Unfortunately, today it is difficult to trace the presence of domestic slaves in Richmond homes of lesser scale. Many of these houses have been demolished, and the associated outbuildings that may have housed one or two African Americans have vanished as well. It is likely that servants of this type of smaller household lived off the premises, boarding with

The Elizabeth Van Lew Mansion at 2301 East Grace Street (demolished, 1911) was the birthplace of Maggie Walker and typical of the high-style "urban plantations." *Author's collection.*

other slaves and free blacks in the teeming shantytown of African American housing that was common in Shockoe Valley. Poverty contributed to the degradation of the architecture associated with this stratum of society; nearly the entire world of domestic architecture associated with slavery has been erased.

Black women were more likely to be employed by families of more modest means who could not afford the investment of housing a slave, let alone owning one.[22] Early morning in Richmond probably saw large groups of African American women toiling up Church Hill or Shockoe Hill to their employment as either hired slaves or free persons for another day of service in the homes of white Richmond.

They may have passed their male relatives making their way toward the mills or tobacco factories, where others joined the commute from each alley and tiny side street of Jackson Ward or the upper end of Shockoe Valley. This tide of workers, along with all the other traffic that circulated through the dusty streets of the city, rolled on year after year. To the north, beyond the poorhouses and hovels, beyond even the sound of the bells of St. John's Church, the storm that was a civil war was about to descend on Richmond and all its inhabitants, rich and poor, free and enslaved and black and white alike.

The conversion of Richmond from industrial center to armed camp, and from the capital of Virginia to the capital of the Confederacy, only increased the hardships felt by blacks. African Americans had to endure the difficulties shared by the whole population of the besieged Confederate capital, such as shortages of food and clothing. In addition, blacks came under greater scrutiny and their movements were restricted as an air of wartime suspicion increased. Confederate leaders believed blacks to be increasingly defiant and the old rumor of slave insurrections once again filtered through the streets of Richmond, even to the office of President Jefferson Davis.[23]

Public whippings became more common under the tenure of Mayor Joseph Mayo with his penchant for order in the face of wartime emergency. Slaves and free blacks alike were subject to arrest and the humiliation of the public whipping post. Both groups were also impressed to work on the fortifications around Richmond.[24]

Under the leadership of General Robert E. Lee, these trenches, forts and gun emplacements took the form of three rings of earthworks in a forty-mile arc around the city. Lee, whose background was that of a military engineer, became known as "the King of Spades" for his tireless construction of Richmond's defenses.[25] At the beginning of the war, two thousand men were recruited to work on the lines around the city. By 1864, the number reached ten thousand and the provost marshal arrested blacks in the streets of Richmond and sent them to work on Richmond's defenses.[26] The resources consumed by the creation of these structures were enormous. Not only did tons of dirt have to be moved, shaped and dug by hand, but hundreds of acres of land also had to be stripped in order to create fields of fire and vast amounts of timber and boards had to be cut and sawed to build the necessary structures to shelter troops. Providing even minimal rations and shelter for the slaves and free blacks forced to work on the fortifications was the equivalent of maintaining a separate army.

Today the hand of time has softened the landscape in and around Richmond, and development of the suburbs has covered much of the former battlefields where African

Americans toiled, building the dikes that held this reservoir of blacks in bondage. Although surviving earthworks can still be found inside the city limits, only period photographs of the extensive fortifications around the city can do justice to the enormity of this task, which was almost completely performed by African Americans.

An example of a Civil War fort, no doubt constructed by black hands, is on Canterbury Road, hidden in the Windsor Farms area of the city. This ring after ring of trenches, forts, ditches, roads and dugouts can rightly be termed the architecture of war, and its purpose transformed the landscape around the Confederate capital. The fact is that these earthworks were built almost exclusively by Richmond black men and formed occupations for hundreds of them. All this was achieved in an effort to protect the institution that enslaved them—an irony likely apparent to all.

The demand for more laborers in Richmond became intense with the beginning of the Civil War, and the antebellum normality of the city was lost forever.

> *The Confederate war machine required slave labor to build its fortifications, work its factories, quarry its mines, fix its railroads, defend its harbors, tend its urban areas, and serve its soldiers.*[27]

The influx of soldiers, bureaucrats, refugees and prisoners no doubt drove the African American residents of Richmond, slave and free alike, into housing of lesser and lesser quality as the quarters and tenements they once occupied were taken over by newcomers to the Confederate capital.

> *Thousands of slave residents performed many, if not most, of the non-combatant tasks throughout the four years. Initially many became involved in the war effort through the hiring out system. Later, impressment laws kept them working.*[28]

Such was the demand for slave workers; the Confederate government began to commandeer slaves, first to dig fortifications. White workers in factories and mills left the city for army service, creating more gaps in the ranks of industrial laborers. As the emergency increased and more blacks were needed, laws were enacted dictating mandatory service for sixty days in the service of the Confederacy and African American criminals were sentenced to labor instead of prison terms.[29] The effect of this whirlwind of change, besides making the plight of enslaved blacks in Richmond more acute, was that increasing numbers of rural blacks now appeared inside the city and were exposed to the customs and knowledge of urban slavery. Skills were transmitted, connections were made and groups sought mutual protection through church and benevolent organizations. This was a coalition of necessity, because the emergencies of wartime had caused an erosion of the few privileges and freedoms (such as hiring out and freedom of movement) that had been inherent in the system of urban slavery that existed before the war.

The conditions for African Americans in Richmond grew worse and worse with each more desperate month of the Civil War until the storm broke in April 1865. With the fall of Richmond, the slave jails were thrown open and those confined were released into a new and uncertain world of freedom.

Despite being delivered out of bondage, the situation of Richmond's African Americans at the end of the Civil War was dire. Six months after the fall of Richmond, and with the coming of cold weather, a Baptist minister remarked:

> *Those who are at work scarcely get enough to keep body and soul together, while the old slaveholders make them pay high for the houses they live in. It seems impossible for the poor here to live through the coming winter.* [30]

Huge numbers of blacks crowding into the city from plantations and farms combined with the chaotic conditions of the Richmond economy meant that local employers felt they could reduce wages. From this inauspicious beginning, an entire societal system had to be created. For a people who had literally less than nothing, the task was daunting. Admittedly, some free Richmond blacks had attained considerable real estate and other assets. Termed the richest African American in Richmond, Reuben M. West owned $12,000 worth of real estate in the city in 1860, during an era when a modest, one-story home cost approximately $500.[31] West, however, was unique in his acquisition of property. The vast majority of black Richmonders were trying desperately to raise themselves above the level of abject poverty as they emerged from slavery.

A historian specializing in Richmond's period of slavery, Midori Takagi notes the importance of the "secret societies" of blacks, many of which were formed immediately following the Civil War. These associations played a huge role in helping the recently freed black city residents fight for their rights, find jobs, increase wages, improve working conditions and accumulate funds. The societies were possible because of the political and financial skills that urban slave men and women developed through living and working in the city. These new organizations were merely the latest outgrowth of community efforts that had helped Richmond slaves build an independent church; negotiate contracts and working conditions; petition for, purchase or "steal" their freedom; provide for their families; develop political alliances; and maintain their humanity and dignity in the face of bondage. Not surprisingly, the black residents who led these organizations had been respected members of the slave community and were prized for their artisan skills, their power within the church and their financial success.[32]

It is from these increasingly sophisticated secret societies that the germ of what would become a golden age of African American entrepreneurship and self-determination would arise in the years after the Civil War. This drive to create economic success and empowerment (as typified by Maggie Walker's work through the Order of St. Luke) helped shape the face of Richmond and its buildings.

> *One of the most significant ways in which Richmond's African Americans influenced the nature and course of urban development was as a result of their efforts to build their own communities.* [33]

This trend is all the more remarkable since this effort toward community building developed so quickly from the clubs and groups that were clandestinely formed during slavery. In a generation, Richmond blacks moved from servitude on the urban plantation to positions of authority, driving an economy largely centered on the talent and finances found in the Jackson Ward community.

This talent and these finances soon began to change the city's built environment as the hundreds of newly freed people began building their own houses and shops. To be sure, many freed slaves preferred to remain in the outbuildings of the urban plantations they had known from their childhoods, paying rent to their former owners for accommodations. Many others, however, chose to strike out on their own, acquire small plots of land and construct their own houses.

4

Black Entrepreneurs, Designers, Craftsmen and Builders

"The most progressive of any in the United States."
—Richmond Planet

By the end of the Civil War, the country's enslaved black population had experienced some 250 years of bondage. Now, however, Richmond's African Americans, like those throughout America, were poised on the cusp of a new way of life. No longer were their labors exerted for others; rather, they could now be directed toward the goal of self-realization.

Ironically, the 1896 *Plessy v. Ferguson* decision of the Supreme Court, which did so much damage to relationships between the races, in a way helped hasten African Americans' move toward a unique form of racial independence. Because the court had determined that separate but equal facilities and accommodations were legal, the division between whites and blacks deepened. But this divide, which would soon give rise to the notorious Jim Crow laws and accompanying attitudes of the early to mid-twentieth century, brought about a flurry of positive activity in the black community. To the fore came a concerted effort on the part of African Americans to create a separate built environment for themselves. Richmond's black entrepreneurs, architects, contractors, craftsmen and others were soon busy in Richmond's black neighborhoods modifying and enhancing their surroundings.

Daniel J. Farrar Sr., an African American born at the end of the slavery era, was one of the people who had a profound effect on the architecture of the city. Farrar stood at the intersection of fraternal associations, architecture and the social hierarchy of Jackson Ward between Reconstruction and 1920. Farrar followed in the footsteps of his father and grandfather. *African American Architects: A Biographical Dictionary 1865–1946* lists fourteen buildings that Farrar was involved with in the 1890s, either as designer, builder or both. No doubt there were many more whose attribution to Farrar has been lost.[1] In 1893 Farrar was advertising his business (then in partnership with family members) as: "All work done in first-class style and in accordance with the latest architectural designs. First-class Work Guaranteed."[2] Farrar's father Joseph (termed "one of the 'pillars' of Ebenezer Baptist Church") was not only a builder, but also one of the principals in the Virginia Building, Loan and Trust Company.[3] Formed soon after the Civil War, the bank reportedly helped "hundreds of men and women in Richmond" to buy homes.[4] Farrar's career spanned a period of rapid expansion of home ownership by blacks in the city, many of the homes constructed by the son and financed by the elder Farrar. By 1920, significantly more of Richmond's African Americans owned their own homes than at any time before—a development made possible, in part, by the lending patterns of the African American financial institutions located within the black community.[5]

Farrar's connections to fraternal orders were extensive, as might be expected of a businessman of his stature. At his funeral in 1923, his body was escorted from his home at 610 North First Street to Ebenezer Baptist Church by a procession of fraternal members of the Elks society, a special committee of which accompanied the body to Evergreen Cemetery.[6] Farrar was also a Mason, as evidenced by his tombstone. The extent that these connections furthered Farrar's career can only be speculated upon, but in the tightly knit Jackson Ward community, where so many African Americans were members of such groups and clubs, this must have been a valuable business resource. Perhaps bolstered by the same network of church, social organizations and support from African American banks, Farrar's son Daniel Jr. also was a builder, "becoming at least the third generation of Farrars to become a carpenter and contractor."[7]

The Farrar family was typical of the changing demographics of Richmond's black population. The same racial segregation that concentrated money and talent in neighborhoods

This vandalized tombstone once identified the grave of one of Richmond's most important builders, who was responsible for many buildings representative of the golden age of African American architecture in Richmond. *Photo by author.*

such as Jackson Ward also created a new African American middle class of young, educated professionals.

> *By 1890, more than half the Richmond black population had been born since 1865, and two-thirds of the others had been children or young teenagers when emancipated. They had been raised within a cohesive network of black mutual assistance, baptized into black-controlled churches, and educated in all-black classrooms.*[8]

These young men and women organized secret societies as a result of seeing themselves as distinct from other blacks.[9] The groups they formed were not, as had been the case in the days of slavery, a security measure against prying oversight by whites, but were for the purposes of spiritual improvement, financial aid, education or entertainment. At one time over a hundred different secret societies were meeting in the African American neighborhoods of Richmond. These included conventional fraternal groups such as the Masons or Odd Fellows. Some were obviously geared toward labor, such as the Stevedores' Society or the United Laboring Men's Society of Coalfield, while other, more socially oriented groups like the United Sons and Daughters of Love and the Manchester Band of Hope may have been created more toward self-improvement.

The proliferation of these societies was emblematic of the rising black middle class, whose program was described as follows:

> *The black community should support black businesses and professional occupations, especially in institutions that directly served them, and they should promote education by the public schools and apprenticeship.*
>
> *As individuals, blacks should be temperate, hard working, and thrifty. In politics, they should look to educated, articulate, and honest men in the community, those with "pride of race."*[10]

Among the most important of the African American social and financial organizations in Richmond at this period was the United Order of True Reformers, founded in 1881 by the Reverend William W. Browne. Of the popular Richmond fraternal organizations, "the largest by far was the True Reformers, an organization that is little remembered today but pervaded nearly every aspect of community life in black Richmond for three decades."[11] The three-bay Italianate house that was Browne's home, now restored, still stands at 105 West Jackson Street in Jackson Ward and is an important site in African American history on a national scale. In 1889, Browne opened the True Reformers Bank in the parlor of this house, the first black bank chartered in the United States. Browne, his hugely popular fraternal organization and its bank were critical to the shaping of African American architecture in Richmond. By concentrating funds and returning them to the community, the True Reformers Bank "stimulated property holding by African Americans and strengthened the financial integrity of the black community."[12]

The primary means by which the True Reformers influenced the city-building process in Richmond was through the real estate holdings of the order itself. A property inventory

OFFICES AND BANK.

———

Return in Five Days to

OFFICE OF GRAND FOUNTAIN, U. O. T. R.,

604, 606 & 608 N. Second St., RICHMOND, VA.

Old Phone 704.   New Phone 1190.

During Reconstruction, African American business, professional and religious leaders came together to form a number of benevolent and financial societies such as the Grand Fountain United Order of True Reformers, shown here. *Author's collection.*

in 1900 listed twenty-eight properties owned by the order. These holdings were reportedly worth $169,463.85 and included fourteen halls, a main office, seven houses, three farms and a two-story stable, as well as a store and a hotel.[13]

The True Reformers organization became a powerful engine that drove the mercantile and entrepreneurial economy of black Richmond, reporting more than $385,000 in real estate holdings by 1903.[14] The degree of growing black enterprise and the burgeoning African American middle and upper class of Jackson Ward financed new commercial and residential buildings, but the black professionals who needed new offices and stores, and who demanded new homes, were without architectural guidance in the African American community and were forced to rely on white architects. John A. Lankford has been termed "the only African American architect for Richmond's Black community, prior to 1910."[15] Lankford enjoyed a long architectural career and in 1922 became the first African American architect licensed in Virginia.[16] Aside from his considerable work for the United Order of True Reformers, he received commissions all over the Eastern part of the United States, and was described as having "designed, supervised and constructed some of the largest and most costly buildings owned by Negroes in America, and many for other races."[17]

In 1892 Booker T. Washington, president of the Tuskegee Institute, introduced architectural drawing to that institution and laid the groundwork for what was to become the architectural program at his school.[18] Washington's influence in creating a pool of professional black architects was critical. A 1901 article by Emmett J. Scott, one of the first published on the subject of African American architects, noted that although blacks had traditionally been employed as skilled carpenters in the American South, black architects were exceedingly rare, and a leading role in the building trade was slipping away from them.[19] Washington's response was to begin with a mechanical drawing curriculum that expanded into electrical engineering, and then a complete architectural program. At Washington's invitation, Lankford left a career as a St. Louis blacksmith, rapidly finishing courses in two trades at Tuskegee. He later earned two master's degrees and taught science at Shaw University. In 1902, at the age of twenty-eight, Lankford was contacted by the Grand Fountain United Order of True Reformers in Richmond to build their Washington, D.C. hall, "which building is said to be the largest in the country designed, owned and built by Negroes."[20]

Lankford was among those who felt strongly that the black community should have its own architects to design the buildings that African Americans paid for and used; a sentiment perfectly in tune with the financial philosophy of the True Reformers. Lankford served as the supervising architect for the AME church, an organization that, he argued vehemently, badly needed architectural guidance: "That the African Methodist Episcopal Church has needed architectural supervision for many years is a fact so plain and simple no sane person will dispute."[21] Indeed, the architect expanded on that idea to include all African American churches that could benefit from black designers:

> *It may be well for me to add, however, that it is not only the A.M.E. Church, which is badly in need of architectural supervision, but all of the Negro churches, with probably*

two or three exceptions, and their membership is small, and they are under the supervision of white church leadership and architects, who had had architectural supervision for many years.[22]

Lankford's work for his church (for which he received no compensation) resulted in his designs being constructed in states as far west as Arkansas, and one Lankford church was constructed in South Africa.[23] Under the title "Architects Who Have Won Their Way Through Pure Merit," Lankford's work was praised in the pages of the *Richmond Planet*. Editor John Mitchell Jr. reprinted a letter from "the white Democratic paper of Potosi, Missouri, where J.A. Lankford and his brother A.E. Lankford were born." The article describes the competition for the design of a Presbyterian church in Potosi where Lankford and his brother were selected over seven white architects, and concludes the Lankfords' plans "were found to be the most satisfactory in every way over those given by [their] white competitors."[24]

Given these kinds of endorsements (and the lack of competing black architects), it is natural that black businessmen in Richmond who were eager to support black professionalism approached Lankford. He was given several Richmond commissions, including a house for the Reverend D. Webster Davis at 908 North Seventh Street. Davis's house appeared in a 1907 publication called *Souvenir Views: Negro Enterprises & Residences, Richmond, Va.*, which illustrated the achievements of African Americans in Richmond by documenting the buildings where they worked, lived and worshiped.

Davis's large, frame, Queen Anne house is pictured beside a much smaller Italianate two-story house above the caption, "Former and present residence of the Reverend D.W. Davis, Richmond's lecturer and poet."[25] The photographic comparison between Davis's two homes is interesting for several reasons. This image is one of a house designed by Lankford, as it appeared when almost new; it is an important record of his work and ability. The fact that Davis chose to build his home next door to his former residence is a statement about either the compression by racial segregation of the African American population of Richmond in Jackson Ward, or simply Davis's attraction to his location on Seventh Street, or both. The fact that the photograph of this stylish, modern home of "black Richmond's poet laureate"[26] is shown and captioned beside his former residence is a deliberate statement about the progress of Richmond's African American neighborhoods such as Jackson Ward, which is held up in *Souvenir Views* as a showcase of black self-improvement.

An important Lankford commission connected with the True Reformers was a complex of a home and apartment building block at 520–526 North Second Street.[27] The twenty-six-room, Queen Anne–style Taylor house, described in 1910 as "palatial,"[28] was constructed for the Reverend W.L. Taylor, the president of the True Reformers Savings Bank.[29] It later became the lodge building for an African American Elks club. The Taylor home, with its distinctive tile-covered domed tower, still stands, and it appeared in a 2002 guide to Virginia architecture with the notation, "Much of the decorative detail has been lost from this structure, but Lankford's boldly modeled forms, including a dominant tower and projecting bay window, remain."[30] This structure from the career of one of the first professional African American architects in the country is a valuable survivor. The Taylor house, once termed "the largest and most costly Negro residence in the United States,"[31] is currently awaiting reuse appropriate to its importance in the history of Jackson Ward.

While the Taylor house still stands to be studied and admired, Lankford's last Richmond design is the most historically significant. The 1908 Southern Aid Society building at 527 North Second Street was not particularly noteworthy from a design standpoint, having a conventional first-floor façade below three arched windows and a heavy, bracketed Italianate cornice typical of many other structures in Richmond.

What did make this small office building distinctive is the fact that it was one of the first modern buildings for a Richmond black-owned business. In addition, the Southern Aid Society building was hailed as the first exclusively African American office building in the country, being the result of collaboration between a black patron, architect and contractor.[32] This important and yet largely unknown building has long since been demolished and is one of the many regrettable gaps in the landscape of North Second Street.

The opening of the Southern Aid Society building was hailed in the pages of the *Richmond Planet* as a glittering affair, and the account of the event describes the intense pride felt by the company in its new structure. Editor John Mitchell Jr. was only too happy to report new developments in black achievement in his home in Jackson Ward.

Only the year before, in 1907, the Southern Aid Society had been pictured in *Souvenir Views* as having its headquarters in a small, awninged building that obviously had been built as a shop.[33] The new structure was a dramatic contrast:

> *On last Monday night, the new Home Office of the Southern Aid Society of Virginia, Inc., No. 527 North 2nd Street this city, was a scene of rarest brilliancy. The occasion being the formal opening of their new and magnificent building to the public. Fortune's Orchestra dispersed sweet music while the thousands of visitors filed in, around and out of the spacious new building, each receiving a magazine, a souvenir and the best wishes of the congenial officers of the company.*[34]

The exclusive involvement of African American craftsmen was remarked on in the notice of the opening. The contracting firm Moore and Archer was selected, "our townsman" William Jones did the electrical work and the elaborate gold lettering that graced the plate-glass windows was executed by "our townsman" George A. Cobbs, a contractor in painting whose work "is in itself a monument of Negro skill and art, and for ages to come will stand out in bold defiance and challenge the world in defense of his genius."[35] Unfortunately, Cobbs's work at the Southern Aid Society building was lost long ago, but it can still be seen in promotional postcards issued by Southern Aid. The memory of Lankford's building, once hailed as "the most modern building owned and occupied exclusively as an office building by Negroes in the United States," remains as a monument to Lankford's ability to give stature and grace to a small commercial building. It is also important to remember that the Southern Aid building was emblematic of the pride and spirit of black enterprise that once energized Jackson Ward.

When Lankford designed the True Reformers Hall in Washington, D.C., in 1902, he used the Richmond True Reformers Hall at 604 North Second Street as a model.[36] The Richmond building was evidently such a success that Lankford was directed by the Order to make it the model for the Washington facility. Together these two buildings represent examples of what has been termed a unique building type: the African American multipurpose building, which provided auditorium, retail spaces and offices. This form became popular across the country and is believed to have had its origin in Richmond with the True Reformers Hall.[37] Maggie Walker used the same concept of a combination of services and facilities with the extensive remodeling of the St. Luke Building in 1919 under the design of Charles Russell.

Built 1891–95, the True Reformers Hall in Richmond was the inspiration of William Washington Browne, leader of the Grand Fountain United Order of True Reformers, who saw the hall not only as a practical building for the organization but also as a monument to the spirit of black self-reliance that the True Reformers promoted.[38] The auditorium space was badly needed by African Americans in Richmond when churches and smaller halls proved to be either inadequate or inappropriate venues, and there were certainly numerous societies that were in need of meeting space.[39] Because it was constructed before the advent of professional black architects in Richmond, Browne turned to Bernard J. Black, an experienced white Richmond architect.[40] Actual construction of the True Reformers Hall was contracted to George Boyd, "one of Richmond's leading African American builders."[41]

Now demolished, the Southern Aid Society building in Jackson Ward opened in 1908. Designed by John Lankford, it was built by black contractors and is believed to be the first African American chartered insurance company in the South. *Author's collection.*

The W.W. Browne House at 105 West Jackson Street is the site of the first black bank chartered in America. This restored house is a landmark in African American history in Richmond because the bank founded here stimulated economic development in the black community.

The True Reformers Hall, with its paired granite-arched Italianate windows and tower, was a commanding presence on Second Street before its demolition in 1955. It was the venue for many entertainments and meetings, among the most important being a speech given by Marcus Garvey, the black separatist and philosopher. Garvey filled the True Reformers Hall on June 30, 1922, and spoke expansively about his plan for blacks to return to Africa.[42] True Reformers Hall hosted many orators, orchestras and balls before being torn down. Its unworthy successor on the site is a motel that is now derelict and awaiting demolition.[43]

The now-vanished African American neighborhood of Fulton, discussed more fully in Chapter Eight, had its own neighborhood version of True Reformers Hall, a two-story frame building with stores and a meeting hall above, but on a much smaller scale. This Italianate-style structure was built between 1887 and 1895 and probably stood until the destruction of Fulton in the 1970s.[44]

The building is credited to Farrar, who may have both designed and built this hall. One of the grander Richmond houses that Farrar constructed still stands at 1401 West Leigh Street, a large brick mansion that once belonged to Ruben Thomas Hill, and a structure that gained much attention during the collapse of the True Reformers Bank in 1910.[45] This handsome Queen Anne–style house, with its large tower and belt courses of granite, was a visual statement about the owner's stability and high status as a bank official. Hill served in a number of positions of trust in the African American community, such as president of the Virginia Baptist Sunday School Convention and president of the Capitol Shoe and Supply Company, and he was about to enter the real estate business at the time of his disgrace and disappearance.[46]

Hill was also cashier of the True Reformers Bank and had been one of the founders of the *Richmond Planet* and the business manager of the newspaper during its early days.[47]

The *Richmond Planet* covered the calamity of the collapse of the Order with headlines reading "True Reformers' Bank Closes. Frightful Crash in Veteran Institution—The Order in Distress—Right to Do Business Revoked. Depositors Will Not Lose Much Money. Order Stranded."[48] It was later revealed that the destruction of the bank was due largely to embezzlement and mismanagement by officers of the bank including cashier Hill, who fled the city.

As the manhunt for Hill was covered in the *Richmond Planet*, the True Reformers Bank attempted to recover from the loss but instead went into receivership. The shock of the collapse of this institution was felt all over the East Coast, but particularly in Richmond, where most of the officers were, like Hill, prominent members of the community.[49] Church members emerging from Moore Street Baptist Church in the Carver neighborhood must have glanced across Leigh Street with dismay at the Hill house, now a symbol of culpability and betrayal. The collapse of the True Reformers Bank financially ruined many African Americans in Richmond and sent economic shockwaves throughout the South.

Hill was never captured and was rumored to have fled to Canada, leaving his family to try to salvage the family home on Leigh Street.[50] Hill's sons and wife "succeeded in saving the palatial home at 1401 West Leigh Street. It was purchased by the family for seven thousand, three hundred dollars," reported the *Richmond Planet*.[51] The house still stands solidly on Leigh Street just as Farrar built it, even if the crimes of its owner rocked the foundations of the African American community in Richmond.

In the wake of the collapse of the True Reformers Bank, John Mitchell rushed to assure the public of the solidity of his institution, the Mechanics' Savings Bank. Large notices appeared in the *Richmond Planet*, with a photograph of Mitchell standing beside a massive vault door.

There has been no run on the Mechanics' Saving Bank of Richmond, Virginia. We have had Money stacked up on our counters to hand out to Timid Depositors, who may be uneasy, but the money is there now. They didn't want it, because they knew they could get it for the asking.[52]

Built by Daniel Farrar for the True Reformers' cashier Ruben Thomas Hill, this palatial house at 1401 West Leigh Street was the Hill family residence at the time of Hill's disgrace and disappearance. Hill's embezzlement led to the failure of the True Reformers Bank.

Mitchell and his institution survived a period of disenchantment with black banks after the downfall of the True Reformers Bank, and became very successful for many years.

The Mechanics' Savings Bank opened in 1902, a byproduct of Mitchell's involvement in the Knights of Pythias, a fraternal organization that he headed under the title grand chancellor.[53] The highly successful Knights of Pythias, with its female counterpoint, the Independent Order of Calanthe, provided the capital to found the Mechanics' Savings Bank. Mitchell began investing in real estate for the bank, acquiring a three-story building at 310 East Broad Street.[54] The Mechanics' Saving Bank was housed for a period in a typical Jackson Ward townhouse, which is pictured in *Souvenir Views* under the title "The Old Pythian Hall and Mechanics' Saving Bank."[55] The conversion of the housing stock into businesses was not uncommon, and many examples of this architecture by necessity survive today on the streets of Jackson Ward.

Altering the front of the house and adding shop windows meant the building was still useful as a private residence, with living quarters upstairs. Mitchell's own newspaper was housed in a townhouse on Fourth Street, its Greek revival front façade partly obscured by a large sign that read "**THE PLANET**," and above that, the newspaper's masthead image of a black man's clenched fist and arm.[56]

Mitchell was not content for his bank to remain in a converted Jackson Ward townhouse, however, feeling that it was imperative that the bank appear "solid, substantial, and secure."[57] Accordingly, he began plans for a bank building at the northwest corner of Third and Clay Streets, noting in February 1909 that "work on the plans for the new Mechanics' Savings Bank is under way."[58] Surprisingly, Mitchell chose a white architect, Carl Ruehrmund, who was experienced at commercial building design, to create the bank. Ruehrmund had designed many major Richmond stores, residences and churches.[59] The choice of Ruehrmund as architect may have been one of practicality, but it also speaks to the shortage of African American architects in Richmond at the time. Had black professionals been available, Mitchell would most likely have used one of them.

The logical choice for a project like this would have been John Lankford, who, as supervising architect of the AME church, Mitchell had praised as "a young Negro architect of much ability and skill, having designed and supervised the best buildings in the country owned by Negroes."[60] Mitchell had a bitter and public feud with W.W. Browne in the 1890s, and Lankford and his designs may simply have been too closely associated with Browne's True Reformers for Mitchell. Also, the absence of Lankford in Mitchell's bank building design may have been due to the prolific architect simply not being available at the time. Mitchell's biographer, Ann Field Alexander, does not comment on the choice of Ruehrmund for Mitchell's new bank design, and the reasons for his appointment remain unknown.

When Mitchell proudly ran an illustration of his new bank on the front page of the *Richmond Planet* in June 1909, the designer of the building was referred to only as "the architect."[61] The following month found Mitchell diverted by his struggle to build his bank, and there was some doubt that he would be allowed to construct it. The *Richmond Planet* reported with some understatement "quite a commotion has been

John Mitchell's Mechanics' Savings Bank, which opened on the corner of Third and Clay Streets in 1910. The building was enlarged in the 1930s by constructing a double of the original façade. *Photo by author.*

caused by the proposal to erect a banking and office building on the northwest corner of 3rd and Clay Streets."[62]

Farrar, as contractor, filed a set of plans with City Building Inspector Henry Beck's office, a procedure that had been codified only two years before.[63] The other property owners on Clay Street (who were all white) filed an objection to Mitchell's plans, saying that his building should conform to the established building setback line followed by the residences on the street. This was a clear attempt to legislate Mitchell's building out of existence, as a fifteen-foot setback on a thirty-foot-wide building would effectively prevent it from being built. Building Inspector Beck stalled, saying that he had not had time to inspect the plans. Mitchell countered in what was apparently a ploy to force Beck's hand. The *Richmond Planet* editor and banker visited Beck in his office and told him that he would apply for a permit to build his bank at Adams and Cary Streets, across from the white Methodist church. In a two-pronged approach, Mitchell revealed plans to put a "private sanitarium (Negro Hospital)" on the site at Third and Clay Streets. The *Richmond Planet* reprinted this account from the *Times-Dispatch*, concluding that the news of the proposed hospital for blacks amid the white residents of Clay Street had the desired effect:

> *This seemed to have caused lively interest even in the office of the Building Inspector, who was free to say that he could not see any reason for objecting to the erection of a banking building on 3rd and Clay streets.*[64]

The following week found Mitchell appearing before the committee on streets at a hearing to determine the fate of his building permit application. The *Richmond Planet* triumphantly announced that the "Permit is Issued—Building Inspector Beck Could Wait No Longer" and reported Mitchell's address to the committee:

> He told of his retirement from politics and of his engaging in business and he entreated the liberal-minded white men not to block the progress of the better class of colored people by any restrictive legislation of this character. In glowing language he pictured the beauties of Lee District and Ginter Park, where the white property owners had removed and he now insisted that the colored people should be accorded liberal recognition.

Mr. Mitchell concluded with a stirring appeal to the committee asserting that the colored people under the aid and guidance of the white people of this community were the most progressive of any in the United States.[65]

For the white readers of the *Times-Dispatch* or the black readers of the *Richmond Planet*, Mitchell and his pleading, combined with vague threats of utilizing other addresses in Jackson Ward to ensure his bank on Clay and Third Streets was permitted, must have seemed quite transparent. These were the accepted twists and turns experienced by blacks in Jim Crow–era Richmond as they tried to overcome the entrenched opposition of whites to the expansion of blacks into other areas of the city. "The colored section back of Clay Street has long been congested and limited by the ravine on the north, and has no other means of growth than to the south," admitted the *Times-Dispatch*.[66] Mitchell and his struggles also are emblematic of the inexorable movement of black businesses and homes into all of Jackson Ward and its transformation into an African American neighborhood.

With his various strategies for approval of the building permit, the editor of the *Richmond Planet* won his case with Building Inspector Beck and the committee on streets, gaining approval for the new bank building. By the following October, Mitchell reported that "the work on the new Mechanics' Savings Bank is progressing," while noting the stucco work being done by "the colored plasterers, Messers. Winston and Freeman."[67] The continual emphasis on the use of African American contractors on this project is consistent with the spirit of black self-sufficiency at the time and a philosophy that money generated within the black community should be spent there for services and goods performed and sold by African Americans. Mitchell was one of Richmond's strongest proponents of this philosophy and seldom missed an opportunity to publicize the achievement of African American businessmen and craftsmen.

A year after the fight against the white property owners on Clay Street, Mitchell announced the opening of his new bank. A large reproduction of the architect's rendering of the building appeared on the front page of the *Richmond Planet* over the notation "Carl Ruehrmund, Architect—D.J. Farrar, Builder." Photographs of the enormous round vault door in both closed and open position also were printed.

Mitchell was quite proud of the vault and door and often posed beside it for photographs, symbolic of the solidity of the Mechanics' Savings Bank. Mitchell was presented with a commemorative cup on the occasion, and the building was open to the public until after midnight.

The account in the *Richmond Planet* described the evening:

The inside of the vault, in the language of the ladies, is a dream. Inside the banking room was decorated with palms and cut flowers. The ceiling fairly beamed and glistened with its magnificent radiance. One should think that 5th Avenue, New York had been removed to Richmond.

Automobiles with their chauffeurs puffed on that corner. Mayor D.C. Richardson and members of the board of aldermen and common council came to see this remarkable production. They went from the basement to the roof and enjoyed themselves. It was 12:30 a.m. when the last word was said, and during the whole evening nothing happened to mar the affair.[68]

The issue of the African American bank on Clay Street set off a legalized attempt to confine blacks to the areas where they currently lived and worked and prevent the kind of expansion that Mitchell had engineered. The Clay Street controversy, combined with a report that the Mechanics' Savings Bank was buying up homes in that part of Jackson Ward, prompted the introduction of a residential racial segregation law in Richmond, designed to freeze existing housing patterns and keep whites and blacks confined to the areas where they currently lived. Mitchell lobbied long and hard against the ordinance, which proved increasingly difficult to administer.

In 1914, members of a black Methodist church at Fifth and Leigh Streets were caught in the complexities of this attempt to confine Jackson Ward blacks. The congregation cut an entrance in their new church on Fifth Street (predominantly black) so as to avoid using the Leigh Street entrance on a predominantly white street. The ordinance was appealed all the way to the United States Supreme Court, which struck down a similar law as unconstitutional. It would be 1917 before the African American members of Leigh Street Methodist Church could use the front entrance of their church.[69]

Jim Crow laws and racial segregation in Richmond were a reality that touched the lives of all of the city's residents, black and white. So pervasive was the attempt to legislate confinement and separation of the African American residents of Richmond that it even affected the character and design of buildings. The protocol of "colored only" and segregated lavatories was a constant reminder of the divisions that crossed the city, fissures that were written not only in the law books but also in the very fabric of the architecture that surrounded Richmond's citizens. The story of the congregation of Leigh Street Methodist Church and their attempts to worship at the corner of Fifth and Leigh Streets is but one attempt to compromise and conform to the harsh reality of the racially divided Richmond of the day.

After years of some success, Mitchell's bank failed in 1922, leaving him penniless. The downfall of the Mechanics' Savings Bank has been attributed to Mitchell's attempt to promote African American business in Richmond. "Mitchell had a good grasp of the real estate market, but his very success got him in trouble."[70] His policy of investing in real estate for black businesses was intended to make African Americans economically independent of whites, but the accounting methods he used could not withstand close scrutiny from the

John Mitchell Jr. (1863–1929). This prominent Richmond businessman and editor of the *Richmond Planet* was a leader in black enterprise and a tireless defender of the city's African Americans and their rights. *Courtesy Library of Virginia.*

State Corporation Commission. Mitchell tried desperately to salvage the bank and even though he sold his own possessions to keep the Mechanics' Savings Bank from bankruptcy, it never reopened its doors.[71]

In 1925 the bank building was sold to a local fraternal organization, and the grandeur of which Mitchell had written so glowingly faded under coats of paint. An interesting tribute to the design of the building was paid in 1930. The building was purchased by the Southern Aid Society, one of the oldest African American insurance companies in the United States. It hired Richmond architect Edward F. Sinnott to duplicate the façade of Mitchell's bank on the left side of the original structure.[72]

The resulting building is, in effect, two of the Mechanics' Savings Bank buildings, bound with a new center entrance. If imitation constitutes flattery, Mitchell, the architect Ruehrmund and Mitchell's contractor Farrar would be pleased with the reconfigured building.

Mitchell and Farrar were but two of the figures involved with the tide of black enterprise that swept through the streets of Jackson Ward, transforming the neighborhood with new homes and businesses. During this period large numbers of houses were being built, and real estate companies catering to African American Richmonders advertised extensively in the pages of the *Richmond Planet*. Large, handsome houses like that of Hill and other members of the black professional elite sprang up. Driven by demand from the affluent professional class, Jackson Ward acquired an architectural sophistication. For example, Charles Russell transformed Maggie Walker's Leigh Street house into a distinctive residence.

In 1904 Mitchell purchased 515 North Third Street, a typical Jackson Ward brick townhouse with the cast-iron decoration around the porch that is one of the architectural signatures of the neighborhood.[73] Mid-twentieth-century westward expansion threatened to destroy the entire block where Mitchell once lived. There was an outcry for the preservation of the house of the *Richmond Planet*'s famous "fighting editor," as he was known. While the homes of his Third Street neighbors were demolished at the end of the twentieth century to make way for the Richmond Convention Center, Mitchell's house and adjacent residences were saved and now stand at 621 and 623 North Third Street.

What would Mitchell think, standing at the cast-iron railing of his house today? He would certainly be familiar with Bethel AME Church, now across the street, but the vistas up and down Third Street would be quite different. The sterile streetscape of the west side of the Richmond Convention Center would be foreign to him, as would the glass and concrete fronts of the laboratory and office buildings of the Virginia Biotechnology and Research Park to the north and east.

Today Mitchell's house stands isolated, a token survivor of a demolished city block. Although its context as a nineteenth-century building was completely lost when its original neighborhood was bulldozed and no signage identifies it, Mitchell's house nevertheless exhibits a stubborn persistence that he would certainly have admired.

While no longer standing in its vanished part of Jackson Ward, Mitchell's relocated house is a fitting and defiant memorial to him as one of the great figures of the golden age of black enterprise in Richmond. His influence on the face of the city, like that of Farrar and countless other black entrepreneurs, businessmen, craftsmen and builders, has yet to be fully appreciated.

5

The New Architects at Work

Jackson Ward and Church Hill

"I secured and read many books on architecture."
—*Charles T. Russell, Architect*

The Jackson Ward cityscape in the first decades of the twentieth century was transformed by African American enterprise. Charles T. Russell, the city's first resident African American architect, helped transform Jackson Ward, which was often called the "black Wall Street of America," from a largely residential neighborhood to an entrepreneurial zone. From Russell's drawings most of the major buildings constructed by and for African Americans in Richmond were built, usually with black contractors and craftsmen.

Russell was fortunate to begin his practice at the high point of this period of affluence, interpreting many of the architectural needs of black business and community leaders of his day. Although his architectural firm did design buildings outside of Richmond, he is best known for his commissions within Jackson Ward.

Many of Russell's buildings have been lost in the erosion of the Jackson Ward neighborhood by the widening of Chamberlayne Avenue and the construction of the Richmond–Petersburg Turnpike (now Interstate 95). This gradual reduction of the neighborhood has in recent years also taken several blocks of important structures from the east side of Jackson Ward for the Richmond Convention Center complex.

Despite this type of wholesale demolition, many of the buildings designed by Russell still stand. These are important structures from the drawing board of an African American pioneer in the architectural field and help illustrate a period of black enterprise and patronage from the black elites who worked and thrived in Richmond in the early years of the twentieth century.[1]

Russell was a graduate of the Hampton Institute in Hampton, Virginia, in the class of 1899, receiving certificates from the carpentry department as well as a diploma from the academic department. The skills he developed at Hampton led to an appointment as supervisor of carpentry at Alabama's Tuskegee Institute in 1901. While teaching carpentry, Russell practiced mechanical drawing and served an architectural apprenticeship during the construction of the Tuskegee campus, termed the largest African American building project in the country.[2] Russell credited much of his architectural education to sources beyond the classroom and recalled in 1923:

I made a specialty of making working drawings such as were necessary for construction purposes (from architect's drawings). My continuous contact with several architects (graduates of the best Architectural schools in the country) gave me considerable advantage. During this time I secured and read many valuable books on Architecture, such as used in the best Architectural Schools. [I also] subscribed to Architectural and Building Journals.[3]

In 1907, Russell was appointed to the staff of Virginia Union University (VUU) as an instructor in manual training and superintendent of the university grounds. VUU provided the base from which Russell was to launch his architectural career, offering steady

This vintage postcard of Maggie Walker's St. Luke Building at 902 St. James Street shows the building after the 1918 renovations by Charles T. Russell. *Author's collection.*

Located in Richmond's Jackson Ward, the St. Luke Building stands as a testament to the financial and business acumen of Maggie Walker, the bank's founder.

Born in 1875, Charles Thaddeus Russell grew up in Richmond's Jackson Ward. He was the first black person to maintain an architectural practice in Richmond. By 1930, he had designed projects valued at more than $1 million. *Courtesy of Arnold Henderson.*

employment and introductions to the educated and wealthy African American families of Richmond, as well as the cachet of association with the university. With the permission of the president of VUU, Russell began to solicit architectural commissions.[4]

Russell designed Richmond's now-demolished St. Luke Penny Savings Bank for Maggie Walker at First and Marshall Streets in 1910, his first professional commission.[5] This was a three-story building distinguished by a pair of tall, arched windows on each side that illuminated the banking floor and broke the line of a heavy cornice that ran around the building above the first-floor windows. A corner entrance was visible from both directions—a popular design during the period for a commercial building in a busy urban setting. Above the windows the words "St. Luke Penny Savings Bank—Established 1902" proudly signaled the purpose of the bank and made a statement about the length of its continual service. The opening of the St. Luke Penny Savings Bank on October 31, 1911, coincided with the failure of the True Reformers Bank, located just a few blocks away. The new St. Luke Penny Savings Bank building was welcomed as a sign of prosperity and stability in Richmond's African American community.[6]

One of Russell's most handsome neoclassical buildings, also now demolished, was commissioned by a Richmond African American lawyer, J. Thomas Hewin, and stood at 1412 North First Street. Russell designed a combination residence and apartment building for Hewin with a large, two-story veranda on the front façade and projecting wings.[7] This arrangement of combining an apartment building with what would ordinarily be a free-standing house may have had its precedent in 1910 with John Lankford's similar complex for Reverend W.L. Taylor on Second Street.

Like office buildings that featured apartments on the upper floors and organizations that built multipurpose halls with retail and office spaces, many of Russell's structures show a level of innovation and flexibility in design. This type of design maximized the use of small city lots in desirable locations in and around Jackson Ward. Russell's multiuse commercial buildings created opportunities for generating income from ground-floor business, suites of offices above and often a meeting hall on an upper floor. An early example of this building type from Russell is the 1910 Johnson's Hall at 10 East Leigh Street, a combination Masonic lodge, funeral parlor and auditorium. This type of building is believed to be a Richmond innovation, based on the model of the 1895 Reformers Hall at 604–608 North Second Street that was copied extensively across the country. Russell and his older colleague, Lankford, designed these multipurpose buildings for a variety of clients.[8]

The appearance of the Richmond multipurpose building coincided with the popularity of small African American social or fraternal groups that filled church halls and auditoriums all over the city. Those who did not have their own facilities would have welcomed the use of a meeting space such as that offered by the True Reformers Hall. The True Reformers building even offered catering on-site, where a confectionary located in the ground floor advertised "the purest cream" and "annual dinners and suppers furnished at short notice."[9] Buildings such as these were social, business, religious and fraternal centers for the African Americans of the era whose social schedule took many of them to an assortment of large and small meeting rooms all over black neighborhoods in the city. As a native of Jackson

Ward, Russell no doubt would have known from an early age many such meeting places in his neighborhood.

In 1911 Russell designed the Richmond Beneficial Insurance Company building, which still stands at 700 North Second Street. This structure is typical of the multipurpose office building often seen in Jackson Ward, with space for two stores on the first floor and offices above. The building was designed to take advantage of its corner lot by offering an angled front entrance visible from either Jackson or Second Street, and a smaller storefront on the side of the building. The offices of this African American company were on the second and third floors and were accessible by a formal stair hall on the rear of the building. The neoclassical entrance decoration, pilasters and granite quoins in the corners of the insurance company building were a popular style at the time, and conveyed a solid but restrained quality that was appropriate for an insurance company.[10]

The insurance company building is in many ways an abbreviated version of Russell's St. Luke Penny Savings Bank, and each incorporated multiple uses to maximize the investment of the owner. In the case of the bank, apartments on the upper floors help sustain the banking enterprise on the first floor,[11] while the insurance building's two storefronts on the ground floor were below two stories of offices.[12] The contractor for the building was Daniel Farrar Sr., whose reputation for quality construction resulted in several collaborations with the African American architect. As seen in many commissions in Jackson Ward, the use of black architect and black contractor was consistent with the spirit of self-sufficiency in the neighborhood.[13]

Farrar also executed Russell's design for a bank building in 1920 at 702 North Second Street for the Richmond Beneficial Insurance Company, located next to the insurance company's offices.[14] Located on a narrow lot, this building presents a classical front of stone and brick with pilasters flanking the entrance. These two handsome buildings designed by Russell still stand on the edge of the area devastated by Interstate 95. Except for recent inappropriate residential infill, these are the last buildings still remaining on the southern portion of the once-thriving Second Street corridor and they represent a tantalizing suggestion of the scale and numbers of buildings that were lost when the highway bisected Jackson Ward. One of the most dramatic structures built by blacks for blacks in Jackson Ward was the First Battalion, Virginia Volunteers Armory at 122 West Leigh Street. The towers of this castle-like building have enlivened the Jackson Ward skyline since it was constructed in 1895 by the City of Richmond.[15] An armory building for Richmond's blacks had been proposed ten years earlier, but only lobbying by *Richmond Planet* editor John Mitchell Jr. and the commander of the Richmond African American militia, Major Joseph B. Johnson, ensured the necessary approval of city council. Mitchell and Johnson hired a carriage and drove around the city, calling on city council members and personally persuading them to override the mayor's veto of a construction plan for the armory.[16]

Mitchell again became involved with the Volunteers battalion after construction on the building began. The subcontractor for bricklaying was Armstead Walker, Maggie Walker's husband, and a longtime contractor in Richmond. Complaints came from the all-white Bricklayers' Union that the contractor for the building had subcontracted

Built in 1895, the First Battalion, Virginia Volunteers Armory is the oldest armory still standing in Virginia. The building played a role in the lives of African Americans for many decades. It also served as a school, and later, as a reception center for servicemen of color during World War II.

Walker and his black masons for the brickwork. Mitchell made a personal plea before the city council committee that oversaw municipal buildings in an attempt to keep Walker on the job, and succeeded.[17]

Mitchell no doubt realized the importance of what has become known as the Leigh Street Armory for the blacks of Jackson Ward. In the years before the establishment of the National Guard, localities sponsored militia units, which were under the command of the governor and could be called upon by him in the event of an emergency.

The armories where these units were based also served as social centers, being the scene of balls, displays, banquets and fairs. The First Battalion, Virginia Volunteers, had been meeting and drilling in rented rooms since 1876, when the African American unit was established.[18] A permanent home for the battalion volunteers was a major achievement for blacks in Richmond.

Mitchell himself may have been in attendance on October 12, 1895, and written the account in the *Richmond Planet* that detailed the transfer of the keys to the armory from City Engineer W.E. Cutshaw to Major Johnson, commander of the Volunteers battalion.[19] Later that month, Jackson Ward celebrated the opening of the armory with a joyous twelve-day "Military Bazaar" featuring drill competitions, concerts, receptions and refreshments.

"The superb Battalion Band will be in attendance each night to discourse rare selections," reported the *Richmond Planet*.[20]

The importance of this building to African Americans all over Richmond cannot be overestimated. It meant parity with the four white militias in the city on an architectural, social and military level. For the ex-slaves and children of slaves, the sight of armed and uniformed young black men, issuing from this veritable castle in the heart of Jackson Ward, must have been a stirring sight indeed. "On last Wednesday night, the beautifully lighted armory could be seen from this section glowing in magnificent splendor," reported the *Richmond Planet*. "A few minutes past 8 o'clock the tap of a drum told us that the Battalion was about to enter."[21]

The pride of Jackson Ward was not to last long. The discrimination against black troops during the mobilization of the Spanish-American War, along with the overt racism of the Jim Crow era, led to the dissolution of the Volunteers battalion. The Leigh Street Armory was converted into the Monroe School in 1899.[22]

The armory served generations of black Richmond schoolchildren as an elementary school until 1940, when it was described as "an antiquated firetrap."[23] Nevertheless, the building was put back into service for uniformed African Americans during World War II. Renovated and with a gymnasium added to its rear, the building served as the Monroe Service Center.[24] The Richmond Office of Civilian Defense, which oversaw the reception center for black GIs in the former armory building, kept careful statistics and documented that 55,000 African American soldiers spent the night within its walls during the war.[25] Even now, thousands of black veterans all over the United States must recall the hot shower and meal they received when they spent a night in an oddly castle-like building in Richmond, Virginia, during World War II.

After the war, the building continued to be used by the City of Richmond as an annex to nearby Armstrong High School and, later, Graves Middle School. It served for a period in the early 1980s as the Richmond Black History Museum and Cultural Center of Virginia. It was during this time that a devastating fire on the second floor burned off a large part of the roof and made the building uninhabitable.

The Leigh Street Armory languished for more than twenty years as a shuttered ruin, with rain and snow pouring in the roof. In 2003, funds from the National Park Service's "Save America's Treasures" program stabilized the armory and put a new roof on it. It currently awaits a reuse that is sensitive to its unique architectural style and its rich history. This building has enormous significance for African American history in Richmond and for Virginia history in general. It is the oldest armory still standing in the commonwealth and a unique example of an architectural style that has all but disappeared from the American city. It is hoped that the sturdy brick walls erected by black hands over a hundred years ago will soon be reinforced and the "beautifully lighted armory, glowing in magnificent splendor," will again grace Jackson Ward as it did in 1895.[26]

South of Jackson Ward, in the Randolph neighborhood of Richmond, a thriving African American community developed around River View Baptist Church. In 1908, small bungalows were advertised to blacks on Jacquelin Street as available for as little as fifty

Charles T. Russell designed River View Baptist Church in the classical style. It was constructed of reused stones and bricks from a Southern Railway passenger depot.

dollars down and a fifteen-dollar monthly payment. The three-room houses were described as having "nice detached lots, 25 and 30 feet, front porches, galvanized iron cornices, cement wainscoted kitchens, well built and attractive."[27] This neighborhood remains largely African American, but most of the small bungalows pictured in the 1908 advertisement have been demolished in favor of more modern housing or housing developments along the northern edge of the area.

A church in this neighborhood west of Oregon Hill, designed by Charles Russell, clearly demonstrates his ability to work in the classical style of architecture. The former River View Baptist Church is a nicely proportioned, temple-form building at 1525 Jacquelin Street.[28] This church, whose sanctuary stands high above sidewalk level over a tall basement, was designed by Russell in 1914 and built in 1915.[29] The cornerstone notes that the building was "rebuilt" in 1915, a reference to an earlier structure that stood on the site on the corner of Jacquelin and South Lombardy Streets.

Beginning in 1885, the African American congregation had originally worshipped in a nearby house at 426 North Lombardy, then moved to a small, frame building that stood where the 1915 building is today. Russell's church was built of reused material, the brick and stone having come from a Southern Railway passenger depot that stood at Fourteenth and Hull Streets in nearby Manchester.[30] The granite stones that were reconstituted to make this handsome church were no doubt wrested from one of the many quarries that operated along the edge of the James River.

It may have been the same African American workers who tore down the railroad depot and transported the granite stones to River View Baptist Church who would later craft Russell's classical design for their congregation. The architect may well have recalled his work at River View Baptist Church when, some thirty years later, in the 1940s, he was involved with the reconstruction of the carillon and library buildings at VUU. Like River View Baptist Church, this was another structure from a distant site that was reconstituted under his supervision, and in both cases the fragments of the original structure were put to good use in service to the Richmond African American community.

Standing today beside the concrete valley that was driven through the Jackson Ward neighborhood by Interstate 95, the St. Luke Building on the north side of the highway looms over the chasm. Now cut off by the interstate from the main part of Jackson Ward, this building was once the heart of the African American entrepreneurial and humanitarian spirit that galvanized this neighborhood. It still stands as a reminder of the engine of economic empowerment created by Maggie Walker in the early years of the twentieth century, as well as the architectural legacy of Charles Russell.

The St. Luke Building's current dilapidated condition, and that of the disconnected blocks of empty lots that surround it, speak to the decapitating blow Jackson Ward suffered when the highway was built. The building stands at 902 St. James Street on the corner of Baker Street. A *Richmond News Leader* article in 1955 summarized the destruction of the area adjacent to the St. Luke Building and the area known as "Postletown" because of its streets named for the biblical apostles:

> *One stretch of the $69 million turnpike is to pass under Belvidere Street (extended) near Chamberlayne Parkway, and proceed eastward for a distance of about a mile. This stretch will require a 290-foot wide strip, lying between the north curb of Duval Street and the south curb line of Baker Street, and will necessitate the demolition of more than 600 homes, many of them passing a vintage of a century and having housed four generations.*[31]

It is ironic that the building that housed Walker's humanitarian enterprise was cut off from the body of the Jackson Ward neighborhood that she so loved. The vital connection that once existed between the Order of St. Luke and its constituents has been symbolically severed by the dry moat of the highway, and much of the context of Walker's building has been lost. The original structure of the St. Luke Building was a three-story office building designed by John H. White and built in 1903.[32] After the national organization of the Independent Order of St. Luke moved its headquarters from Baltimore to Richmond, the original building was quickly determined to be too small. In 1917 Walker recalled the acquisition of what was then called St. Luke Hall:

> *This $19,090 deal was made...peace and harmony remained in our ranks, and the property now stands on the books of the R.W.G. Council, I.O. of St. Luke, valued at $26,500, corner of St. James and Baker Streets, free of debt, and bringing an interest yearly to the treasury of the organization from this investment.*[33]

Jackson Ward's "Two Street" was the center of business, social life and entertainment for African Americans in segregated Richmond. The area's popular Hippodrome Theater, shown here, was built in the art deco style. To the left is the domed tower of the W.L. Taylor House designed by John Lankford.

The Eggleston Hotel on Jackson Ward's Second Street, an area once known as the "Harlem of the South," accommodated many African American celebrities at a time when white facilities were off limits to blacks.

A large part of Jackson Ward was razed in the 1950s to make way for Interstate 95. The two-story residences in the background are typical of the hundreds of residences that were demolished. *Courtesy Richmond Newspaper, Inc.*

Once used as a segregated city library, this structure at 00 Clay Street now houses the Black History Museum and Cultural Center.

Walker's pride in the St. Luke Building was justified, even in the face of the inadequacy of the new building, since the rapidly growing bureaucracy of the Independent Order of St. Luke demanded even larger facilities.

Realizing that larger quarters were needed, Walker contracted with Russell, who by then had built a successful architectural practice.[34] By the time that renovations were necessary to the St. Luke Building, Russell had designed and supervised construction of numerous buildings on the VUU campus and had as well become the first African American to have an architectural practice based in Virginia. In 1909, Russell applied for an architectural license in Richmond. "Mr. Henry Beck, a Civil Engineer, was Building Inspector at that time," recalled Russell in 1923. "I had no difficulty in meeting the requirements of that office."[35]

Russell expanded and refurbished the existing St. Luke Building in 1918–19 for Walker, adding another floor and expanding the front façade by one bay at the cost of $98,000.[36] The resulting four-story structure had offices on the top floor, meeting rooms on the third floor, an auditorium on the second floor seating eight hundred and the offices of the *St. Luke Herald* newspaper on the ground floor. The basement housed the presses on which the newspaper was printed. Walker's biographer noted that of the three hundred men who worked on the St. Luke Building during Russell's renovation, half were African Americans.[37]

Photographs taken in 1917 for an Independent Order of St. Luke publication celebrating their fiftieth anniversary show the amount of activity that was taking place on the various floors of this building. The white-bloused staff members are pictured in their offices: "Correspondence Office, Accounting Room, Stenographer's Office, Walker's Private Office, Press Room Printing Office, Supply Room, *St. Luke Herald* Office, Juvenile Office, Composing Room, Printing Office." There was also a view of the basement linotype machine and its operator. For group portraits, chairs were brought out onto the sidewalk in front of the distinctive building, and the staff of the Independent Order of St. Luke proudly posed with Walker.[38]

The National Register of Historic Places offers an interesting look at the St. Luke Building as it appeared in 1981, almost fifty years after Walker's death. The document notes that the interior of the building is "remarkably well preserved" and indeed, photographs that accompany the National Register documents show the interior furnished in much the same way as it appeared in the 1917 publication. "The office of Maggie Walker, longtime head of the Order, is preserved as it was at the time of her death in 1934. It retains her desk, adding machine, and bookcases."[39]

The furniture from the building that was noted in the 1981 survey was, unfortunately, sold, but the building retains much of the fabric that Walker and Russell created to serve the once-prodigious demands of the St. Luke organization. The vault of the St. Luke bank that once held the cash and record of deposits of so many Richmond African Americans is still there, although its shelves are now bare. Through gaps in the dropped acoustic tile ceiling installed by later tenants, the magnificent pressed metal ceilings are still visible, and the teller's cage where payments were once collected is still in place. Retractable wood panels that divided meeting rooms, much like today's modular conference spaces, still slide down from the ceilings.

Born on Church Hill in the home of Union spy Elizabeth Van Lew, Maggie L. Walker was the first woman in the United States to charter and serve as president of a bank. In addition to the St. Luke Penny Savings Bank, which opened in 1903, Walker founded a newspaper, the *St. Luke Herald*.

The room on the west side of the building where Walker was frequently photographed at work and where she looked out over the rooftops of Jackson Ward is still in place, although the paint is peeling and many windows have been broken by vandals. The St. Luke Building has been in a state of decline since the 1981 survey, but its potential for celebrating the spirit of African American economic power is undimmed, and the current owner has plans in place for Walker's St. Luke Building to again assume a role in Richmond's economic development.

In 1936, Walker's name was attached to another important element of the Richmond cityscape. A handsome art deco high school, designed by the Richmond architectural firm of Carneal, Johnston and Wright, was constructed at 1000 North Lombardy Street and was named for Walker. The new school was constructed on the site of the Hartshorn Memorial College, the African American school for women that was incorporated into VUU.[40] The building was dedicated in a ceremony held in August 1937.[41] The school had a long and distinguished history of service to African American students until 1989, when it was declared surplus by the city.[42] The structure then sat vacant for almost ten years, much to the dismay of Richmonders who saw the broken windows and graffiti that covered what was once a source of pride of the Jackson Ward neighborhood.

In 1998, the Maggie Walker High School building was renovated to house the Maggie L. Walker Governor's School for Government and International Studies. This is an innovative school offering a college preparatory program emphasizing government, international studies, science, mathematics, languages and fine arts. The comprehensive nature of the institution now housed in her former high school would no doubt be very pleasing to its namesake and, in a happy turn of events, is now a fitting memorial to Jackson Ward's most famous daughter.[43]

Walker's business empire eventually collapsed as the Jackson Ward neighborhood she loved was decimated by the same highway that helped destroy nearby Navy Hill. Many of the buildings and homes she knew have been lost to both neglect and demolition. Another institution from outside Richmond recently acquired the bank she established in 1903.[44] For many years the high school that bore her name was left to deteriorate, and even now her grave in Evergreen Cemetery is overgrown and seldom visited. Nevertheless, one important structure associated with Walker remains in good condition: her house at 110½ East Leigh Street stands as a memorial to the golden age of African American enterprise in Richmond. Certainly no structure in Jackson Ward today affords a better-preserved glimpse of the neighborhood as it appeared in the first decades of the last century. The house remained in Walker's family after her death in 1934. Preserved as the Maggie Walker Historical Site by the National Park Service, which purchased the house in 1979, the house is filled with the furniture and decorations that Walker knew.[45]

Originally built by African American contractor George Boyd in 1889, the Italianate townhouse was later altered by Russell to Walker's specifications, adding a library and a substantial two-story front porch from which the lively world of Jackson Ward could be enjoyed.[46] As Walker's health and mobility declined, Russell also engineered an elevator to serve the second floor. Walker's house is part of what is known locally as "Quality Row," which was home to many of Richmond's elite black society members in the early 1900s.

Maggie Walker High School, built in 1936 in the art deco style, honored the highly successful African American female banker and businesswoman. After many years of being vacant, it recently underwent a $22 million renovation and was restored to its original splendor.

These townhouses could be termed the Park Avenue of upper-class African Americans, compared to the "black Wall Street" only a few blocks to the west. Walker's neighbors on Quality Row in the 1920s included: next door at 112 East Leigh Street, the Reverend J. Andrews Bowler, a Richmond educator who also founded Mt. Olivet Baptist Church; and one door west, at 114 East Leigh Street, Lillian H. Payne, another friend of Walker's and a fellow officer in the Order of St. Luke.[47]

Because so many of Walker's furnishings, books and belongings were preserved by family members, many of the spaces in her house on Leigh Street are retained as she knew them. Inside the rooms, still decorated in ornate Victorian style, the heat and noise of the street are shut out by beaded curtains. A wheelchair much like the one Walker used is parked in a corner of a front room below a portrait of her, made in the same spot. The library is still fitted with her glass-front bookshelves filled with American classics. All along the picture rail, photographs of leading African Americans look down on Walker's various awards and diplomas, while upstairs the living areas appear as though the black businesswoman has simply gone to her office in the St. Luke Building and will return at the end of the day. The architecture and very fabric of the Walker house reflect the presence and use of the strong personality that shaped African American society and business in Richmond.

Upstairs, a rear hallway has been modified and a corner of the wall cut to accommodate Walker's wheelchair as she swung herself down the corridor leading to her parlor and bedroom. A guide points out a skylight above the stairwell, a safety measure installed by Walker after a tumble down the dimly lit stairs so the misstep would not befall another family member. So specific are some of the modifications to the Walker house that it becomes easy to visualize the banker and her architect walking through the halls, discussing what might be done to make the house more efficient and comfortable.

The guides who conduct visitors through the richly appointed rooms at 110½ East Leigh Street point out the electric fixtures, an early addition in a city where most homes, black and white alike, did not have electric lights. The point is made that this degree of sophistication and opulence was not just the reward of a successful businesswoman. The effect of this comparative luxury and style was also to inspire others to follow Walker's admonitions to save money, to invest and to subsequently prosper. Russell, under Walker's direction, turned a townhouse like the others of Quality Row into a comfortable showplace and an example of the power of financial independence.

Walker commanded the resources and connections within the black business community to modify her Jackson Ward home to suit her needs. The space of the entire lot was used in her building campaign to compose a stylish model for her constituents, a comfortable home for her family and accommodations for her driver and his family. The house is inseparable from the woman, and as such, remains a powerful document precisely preserving the life of this important figure and the height of black capitalism in Richmond.

Built in 1889 by African American contractor George Boyd, Maggie Walker's Italianate house on "Quality Row" in Jackson Ward was later altered by architect Charles T. Russell. He added a library and a two-story front porch.

One of Walker's contemporaries was Alfred D. Price, a funeral home director described as "a consummate entrepreneur."[48] The complex of buildings that this enterprising African American built on Leigh Street was within sight of the Walker home, and the black-draped hearses and limousines from Price's considerable fleet must have been a common sight in Jackson Ward. In 1902 Price built a three-story structure that still stands at 212 East Leigh Street, part of a complex of buildings (some of which have been demolished) that played an important role in the social lives of the blacks of Jackson Ward. While the first floor held the funeral business and associated livery stables, the two upper floors held "many elaborately decorated halls and rooms."[49] As was typical with Richmond's black elite, when in 1913 Price needed a new livery stable, he hired Russell to design this utilitarian structure. It still stands behind the former Price facility at 208 East Leigh Street.[50]

Also located in Jackson Ward is a house designed by Russell that is somewhat of an anomaly. Built in 1915 at 508 St. James Street for Dr. W.H. Hughes, this large foursquare-style home is more common in a suburban setting such as Woodland Heights (in south Richmond) or Frederick Douglass Court. The Hughes house is historically significant, but not just because it is a product of Russell's drafting table.

After being conveyed by the Hughes family in 1949, the property was converted into the Negro Training Center for the Blind, the only public school for blind African Americans in Virginia. To accommodate the growing needs of the training center, the property was expanded in 1952 into the two adjoining lots and a large addition was added that, combined with the structure, totals nearly ten thousand square feet. The training center eventually became the Commission for the Visually Handicapped and was used by the group until 1970.[51] The fact that this house, so much in the style of suburban homes of the wealthy, was placed in the heart of Jackson Ward testifies to the desirability of the neighborhood for Richmond's black upper class and the concentration of African American wealth and enterprise in Jackson Ward. The Hughes house may also hint at the difficulty of finding a comparable house in segregated Richmond at the time. The Hughes house has been standing vacant for years, covered with vines and awaiting a suitable reuse on its expansive lot in the heart of Jackson Ward.

Russell's long career came to an end with a design for a Richmond restaurant in 1948, four years before his death in 1952.[52] Known to many as "Czar Russell,"[53] the architect's talents made an enormous contribution to the built environment of African Americans in Richmond. In addition to his abilities as an architect, his achievements as an educator of young black men to follow his path should not be overlooked.

One of Russell's students was Harvey Nathaniel Johnson Sr., who was mentored by Russell after they met at what would become VUU.[54] Johnson, who came from a family of carpenters and builders, established an architectural practice in Norfolk after World War I. He eventually designed many homes and churches in Norfolk and Portsmouth. He collaborated with Russell on one of his most famous commissions, the Attucks Theater, a multipurpose theater and office building in Norfolk.[55] Looking back over Johnson's career, his entry in a biographical dictionary of African American architects notes:

Johnson's long and multifaceted career illustrates several patterns shared by many African American architects: they came from families that had experience in construction, their mentors were frequently fellow African Americans, they formed collaborations/partnerships with other African Americans, the majority of their clients were African Americans, and as highly visible professionals they became leaders in their communities.[56]

A list of the senior Johnson's Richmond commissions includes two houses designed by the architect at 102 West Jackson Street for an attorney named J.W. Thompson, and a house at 1115 North Thirty-first Street for a J.P. Wood.[57] The house on West Jackson Street was claimed by the deterioration of that part of Jackson Ward that accompanied the construction of the interstate. The area is now an urban prairie of empty lots. The recently renovated house on North Thirty-first Street still stands as a Richmond townhouse typical of the period.

The area near Johnson's Thirty-first Street commission is an interesting part of the Church Hill north neighborhood; just a few ordinary looking city blocks actually encompass several sites important to African American architectural history. Not far away at Twenty-ninth and Q Streets are the shuttered remains of the once-handsome Robinson Theater. The Robinson, which opened in 1937, was named for Richmond native Bill "Bojangles" Robinson and was built by the Hill Amusement Corporation as a "colored" theater. The builders were James Fox and Sons, the architect Edward F. Sinnott. The theater marked the transformation of this section of Church Hill into a middle-class African American neighborhood. An outline on the front wall marks the spot where a plaque once honored Robinson, "The World's Best Tap Dancer."[58] The opening of the Robinson was an important event for African Americans who lived on Church Hill. The theater signaled parity with white sections of the city, where a number of ornate movie "palaces" were built in the previous decade. Even the fabric of the Robinson Theater was significant for black Richmonders: the signature and footprints of Bill "Bojangles" Robinson were impressed in the sidewalk in front of the theater.

Behind the Robinson Theater is an innocuous looking two-story structure that appears to be a disused warehouse. This building has had an interesting history, but will be of more importance to the African American community on Church Hill in the future. It was built on the corner of Twenty-ninth and P Streets in 1912 as a railroad station for the Richmond and Rappahannock River Railway.[59] The railroad ran north along Twenty-sixth Street and then northeast along Nine Mile Road, where it carried visitors to the site of the Civil War's Seven Days' battles, a popular weekend picnic area in the early part of the twentieth century. The trains also transported agricultural goods to the city. Today, no trace of the station's former use remains, except for what was once the roof over the train platform. In 2005, the City of Richmond purchased it for use as a teen center for the neighborhood.

Today, the glittering marquee of the Robinson Theater that once shone up and down Q Street is gone and only a trace of the building's former glory remains. The theater has been boarded up for years. The footprints and signature of Bojangles Robinson are now barely visible in the concrete and are, like the theater that provided

Dedicated in 1937 by Richmond native Bill "Bojangles" Robinson, the Robinson Theater at 2903 Q Street in Church Hill retains the legendary dancer's footprints and signature in the sidewalk by the front entrance. Designed in the art deco style by Edward F. Sinnott, the building completed the transformation of northern Church Hill into a middle-class African American neighborhood.

so much entertainment for Church Hill residents, a fading memory. Among the former patrons who attended movies at the Robinson was former Virginia governor and current Richmond mayor L. Douglas Wilder. Wilder was six years old when the Robinson opened only a couple of blocks from his home at 933 North Twenty-eighth Street. The Wilder home, built in 1923, has been demolished and his entire former neighborhood has been replaced with small tract houses as part of the urban renewal initiative of the 1960s.[60]

The vanished childhood home of Wilder was designed by Ethel Bailey Furman, one of Church Hill's lesser-known but more important residents. Born in 1893, Furman is credited with being the first female African American architect in Virginia.

The daughter of Madison J. Bailey, the second black contractor to be licensed in Richmond, from childhood Furman led a life defined by architecture and the building arts.[61] As a girl, she would follow her father to building sites, familiarizing herself with building terminology and methods of construction, eventually assuming some of the drafting tasks associated with her father's business.[62] The Bailey home at 3025 Q Street, with its Queen Anne–style tower and distinctive pylon porch supports, was designed and built by Madison Bailey and served as both home and office for him and his daughter. It still stands, one block away from the Robinson Theater.

This house in Church Hill was the residence of the first African American female architect in Virginia. Ethel Bailey Furman gained her architectural knowledge from working with her father, Madison J. Bailey, in his successful contracting business.

Furman is credited with over two hundred architectural commissions. Among those is an educational wing for Fourth Baptist Church at 2800 P Street, almost within sight of the Furman house on Q Street. The architectural history of Fourth Baptist evolved from worship in an abandoned Confederate barracks on Chimborazo Hill in 1865 to the present classical building, constructed in 1884.[63] With a growing congregation, Fourth Baptist Church was in need of larger facilities and naturally called on congregant and neighbor Furman to design an addition to the nineteenth-century sanctuary. The educational wing that Furman designed was a dramatic departure from the architectural program of the original building, being in a linear modernist style with colored panels in contrast to the classicism of the older building. The 1961 educational facility creates a statement by both the architect and her patron that the congregation had architecturally moved into the twentieth century.

Another Furman commission in the immediate vicinity of this important pocket of Church Hill is the baptistery addition to Cedar Street Memorial Baptist Church at 2301 Cedar Street. This was apparently incorporated into the 1975 addition to the western end of the church. The only other currently existing Furman design in Richmond is the St. James Holiness Church at 16 East Twenty-eighth Street in south Richmond. This small, utilitarian chapel, built in 1957, apparently replaced a 1939 structure also designed by Furman that stood next door to the present building.[64]

Much of the neighborhood that Furman knew in Church Hill has been swept away and with it many of the buildings designed by the architect. As one biographer put it:

With some two hundred buildings credited to Furman, it is significant that she has not been included in the architectural discourse in Virginia. Furman's earliest works and published references to her as an architect predate any known female architects and more specifically any Black female architects in Virginia.[65]

Nevertheless, the architect was honored in 1985 by the naming of a small city park in her memory. It is appropriate that this park is located at Twenty-eighth and M Streets, just a few blocks away from her home, her office, Fourth Baptist Church where she worshiped and the neighborhood she knew so well. With time, Furman may be more appreciated as a forerunner in a field where successful women are not common, even today. To have been an African American woman in the early 1900s and to have surmounted this challenge speaks of enormous determination and faith.

To casual observation, the neighborhood around the Furman home is not particularly distinguished architecturally. Where the Wilder house stood to the south, a tidy area of comparatively new houses replaced the original building stock, but otherwise the tall columned façade of Fourth Baptist Church in the distance is the only noteworthy structure. To look deeper, however, reveals the unique character of this area and the important structures that dot the landscape within several blocks: a rare surviving house designed by Harvey Johnson; the site of the home of America's first African American governor; the

Fourth Baptist Church at 2800 P Street, showing the original 1884 building and the international-style educational wing designed in 1961 by Ethel Bailey Furman.

home and office of Virginia's first black female architect; a major commission designed by her that is a wing on the church where she worshipped; a once-imposing art deco theater built for blacks on the eve of World War II; and a former train station rife with potential for service to the African American community. It requires only close examination to peel back the plywood, remove the layers of paint and rust and to see the connecting lines of history and association, structure and personality and building and community that shaped and continue to shape the face of Richmond in its traditionally African American communities.

6

Virginia Union University and Frederick Douglass Court

"The People's Real Estate..."
—*The* Richmond Planet

Brook Road is today a rather ordinary looking thoroughfare into Richmond, one whose path was disrupted in the 1950s by the construction of Interstate 95. The road formerly ran directly through Jackson Ward, where its diagonal path still cuts across the grid of the city blocks to Broad Street. This, once the principal entry into Richmond from the north, has been relegated to secondary status, and Brook Road today serves principally residential and light industrial areas of the city. Along its path, however, are some significant sites of African American architectural history. Several of these are near the distinctive international-style tower of Virginia Union University, Richmond's historically black school of higher learning that abuts Brook Road.

The extraordinary story of VUU, with its improbable beginnings in the former slave jail operated by Robert Lumpkin in Shockoe Valley, is one of achievement against daunting odds. A gauge of its progression through the decades can be seen in the school's architectural record. From a literal low point, both societal and geographical, in the Shockoe Valley slave jail, VUU has risen to a coherent campus of handsome stone and brick buildings. This path from wooden slave jail to the granite halls of higher education is dramatic and reflects the changes Richmond itself has experienced over the last 140 years.

With the support of local African American leaders and clergymen, the school that became VUU progressed rapidly from Lumpkin's Jail to a location in a Main Street hotel. Through a series of mergers with other black institutions of learning, such as the Hartshorn Memorial College (HMC), VUU was created and established at the HMC location at Lombardy Street and Brook Road.[1]

The school is unusual in that, with some modern exceptions, it is centered in almost the same group of buildings where the school began operations in 1899. This collection of late Victorian, Romanesque revival–style buildings originally included nine structures, all designed by Washington architect John H. Coxhead, and all constructed in the 1890s.[2] The use of granite as a material for collegiate architecture conveyed a sense of permanence, while the lively Victorian decorative scheme of the group, with its turrets and rough-hewn ashlar stone façades, was highly stylish for its day.

Virginia Union University and Frederick Douglass Court

This early twentieth-century postcard image shows the elegant main entrance to Virginia Union University, opened in 1899. The university is distinguished by its late Victorian, Romanesque revival granite buildings. *Author's collection.*

An important African American architect left his mark on the campus of VUU, designing the HMC women's dormitory in 1928. Albert I. Cassell was a professor of architecture at Howard University in Washington, D.C., and is largely responsible for the look of the HU campus, having designed many of its buildings over the course of an eighteen-year career there. Cassell's master plan for the Howard campus is credited with creating the popular perception of the university as the "the Harvard of historically black universities," and his stately buildings at Howard emphasize this concept.[3] His dormitory at VUU was a valuable addition to the campus landscape from this important black architect of the mid-1900s.

Charles T. Russell is the most noted African American Richmonder whose name is associated with the architectural program of VUU. Aside from being a professor on the faculty at the school, Russell enjoyed a long association with VUU, which included designing a series of four faculty houses, now demolished, for the university in 1914.[4] He also designed a frame dwelling for the school twelve years later.[5] In addition, Russell is credited with the restoration of several of the first generation of VUU buildings, including Huntley Hall, a five-story dormitory.[6]

Russell's last major work on the VUU campus was as assistant architect on the Belgian Friendship Complex.[7] Now known informally as the Belgian Building, this has become the signature structure of the VUU campus. Originally designed as a pavilion of the 1939 New

York World's Fair, the international-style group of buildings became a gift to VUU from the Belgian government. Its distinctive tower rises above the university and is visible for miles in every direction. Russell retired soon after he helped move the Belgian Building to Richmond in 1942.[8] His importance to African American architecture in Richmond, aside from the buildings he actually designed for blacks, may be in the education he imparted to generations of young men who were trained to be either artisans in the building trade or architects. His legacy may be subtle, but it is probably much more pervasive than has been documented.

John Mitchell Jr. applauded the efforts of Russell's achievement as an African American architect that the black community needed. Mitchell also knew home ownership was fundamental to black self-reliance and economic freedom. Professionals such as Russell confirmed the importance of the built environment for the African American community and moreover signaled a new parity with white businessmen. With Russell, a professional and energetic person, no longer would Richmond's blacks have to rely on white architects to plan the stores and churches and homes of the African American elite.

Mitchell was also vitally interested in homes for the growing black middle class in Richmond, and used his newspaper to promote the concept. A 1905 article in the *Richmond Planet* described home building:

> *It is the work of a lifetime, but is a task full of pleasurable satisfaction…to a man of home loving instincts it is a work which should prove a source of continual pleasure. To the man who loves to provide for the comfort and happiness of his family, no more enjoyable task could be assigned.*[9]

This meditation on construction of the home ran beside an article about a new design of disappearing window sashes and below a regular column called "The Modern Home," which gave a floor plan for "just such a home the man on a small salary would be able to provide for his family."[10]

Mitchell ran notices on the front page of the *Richmond Planet* to encourage home buying by blacks and to detail recent purchases. This type of boosterism encouraged economic investment and interested his readers as local news items. Such news would in no small way help prompt real estate purchases financed by the nearby Mechanics' Savings Bank, which he founded:

> *The colored citizens are buying property and the houses at 2nd and Leigh streets have passed into their possession. Jacob F. Wright has purchased one of the attractive bay window brick dwellings, No. 531 N.*
> *2nd Street. Mr. William H. Johnson purchased another at 535 N. 2nd Street and it is reported that Misses Rosa B. and Lizzie G. Yancy have purchased the other one at 533 N. 2nd Street. The prices ranged from $2,285 to $2,500.*[11]

In 1905, Mitchell ran a list of property for sale by "The Peoples Real Estate and Investment Company" at the top of page one of the *Richmond Planet*, emphasizing the importance of real estate and home ownership in the minds of both the editor of the newspaper and his readership. The fact that the houses listed often have sequential addresses indicates several built by speculators, such as the four homes built at 608–614 North Sixth Street, each priced at $3,500. With the prominence of this notice in his paper, it is hard to imagine there was not some financial connection between Mitchell and the real estate company that handled these properties, some for sale for as little as $400.[12] As an indication of Mitchell's abiding faith in the African American real estate market, when his Mechanics' Savings Bank failed in 1922 it listed over $127,000 in outstanding real estate loans on its books.[13]

The continuing concentration of black wealth, talent and investment in Jackson Ward and pressure on the surrounding blocks of homes led to some dramatic steps by the white establishment in Richmond to contain African American home ownership.

In 1911, an ordinance was passed by city council that no resident, black or white, would be able to move into a city block where the majority of the residents were of the opposite race. A companion bill authorizing the city to investigate annexing parts of Henrico County on Brook Road as a place to develop blocks for African American housing also passed. The Brook Road scheme failed and the United States Supreme Court finally overthrew the racial zoning law in 1917.[14]

The entire episode reflects the nature of the expansion of the African American community during this period and, also, its dissatisfaction with often deteriorating rental properties in Jackson Ward, where the developing black middle class and a majority of renters lived side by side.[15] Moreover, it is also indicative of the growing affluence of Richmond blacks who demanded modern and stylish homes reflecting their status and of the need for professionals such as Charles Russell to serve this growing demographic.

Good examples of the expansion out of the Jackson Ward core can be seen in various sections of the city, some of which were specifically marketed to African American buyers. For example, in 1906 a subdivision on either side of Selden Street in Church Hill, called Woodville, was advertised as "the colored man's paradise." The grandly worded advertisement for Woodville advised:

> *Any colored man buying one of those lots in Woodville while the price is low, will find himself on the road to peace and happiness. Many colored families now own their own houses there and many more will join them soon.*

Among the attractions of "Happy Woodville" that the advertisers were careful to note was that the subdivision was not far from the streetcar line. The appeal of traveling into downtown Richmond by streetcar was a factor in real estate desirability and values for white and black Richmonders alike, and all the more important in far-flung corners of the city such as Woodville. This, combined with the lure of modern houses on lots financed for as little as three dollars per month, made small, new neighborhoods like Woodville very attractive.[16]

Later than Woodville, and a very specific example of the expansion of the black community out from Jackson Ward, is Frederick Douglass Court, located in the area bounded by Brook

Road and Overbrook Road and along Dubois Avenue. This is an important adjunct to the story of African American entrepreneurship in the city that includes Maggie Walker, Jackson Ward and the development of suburban Richmond.

African American speculators laid out this development in 1919 on land adjacent to VUU, Walker being among that "group of friends" who formed the University Realty Company and subdivided the land.[17] Because it was created, marketed and sold by African Americans, prospective lot buyers would not be subjected to the prejudice that so affected the racial composition of neighborhoods and real estate in general in the city. The subdivision also afforded Richmond blacks the same opportunity to escape the urban core of the city and move into a suburban community that was served by the streetcar. This trend to "streetcar suburbs" was seen in areas all over the city as this type of transportation became more and more common. All across Richmond, neighborhoods such as Highland Park on the north side and Woodland Heights on the south side of the James River owe their origins to the convenience of commuting by streetcar.[18]

Frederick Douglass Court was desirable for reasons beyond its location on the streetcar line, although that certainly was an important factor. Being adjacent to VUU implied a certain cachet as a home suitable for educated and fashionable black Richmonders. The same trend of a highly desirable residential area adjacent to a university can be seen

Two houses that were featured in a 1927 description of Frederick Douglass Court have recently been restored.

in the wealthy neighborhoods that abut the grounds of the University of Richmond in Richmond's West End. Indeed, the name of the development company that created Frederick Douglass Court, the University Realty Company, clearly signals the importance of VUU in the concept of the subdivision. The parity with white universities, even to the quality of housing that adjoined college campuses, was not lost on prospective buyers of lots in Frederick Douglass Court. Many of these may have been educators who taught at the nearby university, but even for the layman, the proximity of the university would have given added value to the subdivision and an implication of affluence.

The subdivision was laid out into 113 lots generally 30 by 135 feet, with larger parcels in what are now the 2500 and 2600 blocks of Brook Road. The lots cost between $675 and $825 and could be financed at 6 percent with payments made annually. Interestingly, the developers also offered several models of homes, and their choice of designs must have reflected what they felt represented the architectural tastes and economic buying power of their fellow affluent black Richmonders in the 1920s.

The concept of providing the housing stock for the area must also indicate the close cooperation between the principals of the venture and the builders who would construct the houses that were proposed for Frederick Douglass Court. As described in 1927 in a book titled *Negro Housing in Certain Virginia Cities*, the model homes in Frederick Douglass Court were of three types. Type number one was of the style generally termed "foursquare." This was an economical suburban style found all over the United States and very popular in Richmond at the time. For the price of $6,500 (which included the lot), buyers received a turn-key stucco home with "bath, pantry, Arcola heat [a type of coal furnace], built-in refrigerator, and ironing board, gas range, hot water heater, open fireplace of pressed brick in the living room, walls painted, and floors of number one pine." These middle-priced homes may be the three illustrated in *Negro Housing in Certain Virginia Cities*, which still stand today at 1213–1217 Dubois Avenue.

Of the houses planned to fill the streets of Frederick Douglass Court, type number two was a six-room, two-story, frame and stucco house with all the features of type number one, but added a slate roof, sun parlor, hot water heat and hardwood floors in some rooms. The house at 1210 Overbrook Road fits this description and may be one of these model homes for the neighborhood.[19] If this is correct, these highest-priced homes were and still are very handsome indeed and excellent examples of the foursquare style.

Type number three was more Spartan and smaller in design, without central heat or the other amenities available in type one and two styles. Two examples of this third style of modern home were built side by side at 1234 and 1236 Overbrook Road, and one of them is illustrated in *Negro Housing in Certain Virginia Cities*.[20] They have been recently renovated, and after years of neglect, have again become a real contribution to the fabric of Frederick Douglass Court, looking much as they did when photographed in the 1920s. A walk around the neighborhood today shows that comparatively few of these demonstration houses were built on the lots of Frederick Douglass Court. Indeed, the author of the 1927 book describing the subdivision noted:

Three of the houses built to set the architectural pattern of Frederick Douglass Court, a uniquely African American streetcar suburb.

The prices of the model homes were higher by perhaps 15 percent than their actual values would justify. Sales at these prices have not been and are not likely to be very rapid. There is nothing, however, to prevent a Negro from building his own home in this section at any cost not less than $1,500.[21]

The high pricing of lots in the subdivision may have been a deliberate ploy on the part of the developers in an attempt to ensure that a certain economic level of the African American community would own and build in the neighborhood. The presence of Maggie Walker's fashionable home on the large Brook Road lot she owned would certainly have lent appeal to the neighborhood and offered an attraction that could have justified the higher prices. Walker chose instead to remain in her house at 110 East Leigh Street amid the lively streets of Jackson Ward and never built on the Frederick Douglass Court lot that she once owned.[22]

As early as 1927, Charles Louis Knight, author of *Negro Housing in Certain Virginia Cities*, speculated on the future of Frederick Douglass Court, saying:

The development and sale of this property is in the hands of Negroes, and it will be interesting to see whether they will avail themselves of their opportunity to help members of their race toward home ownership at reasonable prices and terms, or whether they will seek a monopoly profit in preference to other and bigger interests.[23]

The subdivision clearly did not develop as its creators intended, with few taking advantage of the offered house designs and financing. Nevertheless, a core group of upper-class African Americans did leave the busy streets of downtown to live in Frederick Douglass Court.

On the corner of Dubois and Langston Avenues at 1255 Dubois stands a yellow stucco house, which probably represents an example of the more elaborate model homes planned for Frederick Douglass Court. The design is unusual in that blocks that protrude through the stucco façade apparently once accommodated a planter under every window. This house is the childhood home of Justice Spotswood Robinson III (1916–1998), a major figure in the civil rights movement of the 1950s and the neighborhood's most famous resident. Robinson, a 1936 graduate of nearby VUU, rose to prominence as a professor of law and for his work with the National Association for the Advancement of Colored People alongside Thurgood Marshall. Robinson ended his career as a justice of the Ninth Circuit Court of Appeals after having been appointed to the post of federal judge in the state of Washington by President Lyndon Johnson. These were appointments of high distinction for an African American lawyer during this time period, aside from Robinson's important work for civil rights.[24]

Despite his far-flung career that took him to the other side of the United States, and with his many achievements, Robinson never forgot his Richmond home in Frederick Douglass Court. He elected to come back to his old neighborhood late in life. On returning to Richmond, Robinson chose to build a house and live on one of the large Brook Road lots that were intended for the showplace homes of Richmond's black elite, thus helping fulfill the intention of Maggie Walker and her fellow investors in the University Realty Company that these lots and their affluent owners would set the tone for the rest of the subdivision.

Robinson had a keen interest in the built environment and was a tireless woodworker in his basement shop. The home he designed and built at 2500 Brook Road is an interesting and eclectic example of American architecture of the 1950s, integrated into the landscaping with cantilevered porch supports and a belt of grillwork above the principal windows to regulate sunlight. The house is unique, and is a reflection in architecture of the same iconoclastic mind that helped shatter so many racial barriers during the civil rights movement.[25]

An important structure that is not inside the boundaries of Frederick Douglass Court but significantly faces the neighborhood is the former Richmond Community Hospital at 1209 Overbrook Road. This redbrick, art deco building probably furnished employment for African American professionals in the health field who lived nearby in Frederick Douglass Court. Richmond Community Hospital was constructed in 1932 and was the subject of a heartfelt appeal in 1927 to raise funds for what was termed "Richmond's Greatest Need: Build this hospital now."

Richmond owes proper hospitalization to the colored citizens. They do not have it now and this [i]s said not in criticism of the hospitals which are now serving colored people but is based upon facts which are manifest. Thirty-two physicians treating 70% of the colored population of Richmond are denied the opportunity to practice their profession in

The home of Justice Spotswood Robinson at 2500 Brook Road in the Frederick Douglass Court subdivision. Robinson built this distinctive house in 1957 on his return to the neighborhood where he grew up.

any hospital in Richmond. This is a peril to the health of the community which should not be regarded with indifference. In view of its past reputation, Richmond will not fail to correct this condition. Justice, self-respect and loyalty to the best interests of Richmond demand action now.[26]

This urgent appeal illustrates the dire conditions of medical facilities for blacks in Richmond. It also underscores the efforts made in funding and construction of this small hospital on the edge of Frederick Douglass Court. It is an especially noteworthy building in light of its opening in 1932 in the depths of the Great Depression and considering the difficulty of fundraising for its construction and staffing. This timing, and the hospital's presence, is testimony to the sheer determination of the Richmond African American community to have a new health facility. It is also interesting to contrast this facility to the Virginia Commonwealth University Medical Center's West Hospital, built in the same art deco style during the same era, but many times the size of the African American hospital on Overbrook Road. The year the hospital opened is proudly commemorated on the cornerstone.[27] Today the building is part of the VUU campus and is awaiting a new use after Richmond Community Hospital moved to North Twenty-eighth Street in Church

The Richmond Community Hospital at 1209 Overbrook Road. This art deco building was constructed in 1932 after a citywide appeal to raise funds to replace inadequate medical facilities for blacks.

Hill. The story of this earlier building and its significance as an important landmark of African American medical history in Richmond should be kept in mind when the university or a new owner refurbishes it.

Kathryn Reid, a resident of Frederick Douglass Court, lives on Dubois Avenue in a Tudor-style house that she stated was one of the last architectural commissions by Charles T. Russell.[28] Russell was a logical choice as designer of the homes of Richmond's African American business and cultural leaders. His connections to Frederick Douglass Court were many, as he designed houses for prominent Richmond blacks and influenced the architectural program of nearby VUU. He also redesigned the home of Walker, turning it from an ordinary row house into the distinctive home that visitors see today as the Maggie Walker National Historical Site. Russell received numerous commissions from Richmond's African American elite for their commercial buildings and churches as well. A biographer of the architect noted:

> The Black business and professional leaders [of Richmond]…*needed and wanted modern office, commercial and residential structures to replace the old houses and stores that they then occupied. Since these individuals were the beneficiaries of an African American group economy, many of them were eager to patronize African American architects.*[29]

That some, if not many, of the homes in Frederick Douglass Court can be attributed to the leading black architect in Richmond is not surprising. Russell's list of documented architectural commissions is incomplete, but research lists two 1925 commissions for the larger Frederick Douglass Court lots on Brook Road that were never built.[30] Reid's Dubois Avenue home may be one of many undocumented Russell commissions in the area.

A house in Frederick Douglass Court that can positively be attributed to Russell is the one at 2602 Brook Road. This house, built in 1923 for W.A. Jordan, is a stately brick home of the foursquare pattern, with paired windows. W.A. Jordan was president of the Southern Aid Society, one of the oldest African American insurance companies in Richmond and a mainstay on the "Black Wall Street" of Jackson Ward.[31] His brick home is commensurate with his status within the black community as president of an insurance company and as one of the principals of the University Realty Company that developed Frederick Douglass Court. In addition, the Jordan house is of the scale and size appropriate to the larger Brook Road lots of Frederick Douglass Court and has had an addition put on the west side since Charles Russell drew the original plans.[32]

Russell was adroit in various styles ranging from classical to Colonial revival and his use of the Tudor style could be a possibility. The Tudor style was popular in the years before World War II, and was intended to convey a certain solidity and style that signaled an upper-class home. The same style can be found in many wealthier Richmond neighborhoods such as Windsor Farms. Like the choice of Russell as architect, picking a Tudor-style house design for a Frederick Douglass Court home was a logical decision and characteristic of Russell's upscale African American clientele.

The Tudor houses in Frederick Douglass Court at 1244 Overbrook Road and at 1302 Dubois Avenue are similar in design, with their exposed granite decoration and distinctive seam running partially down the length of their chimneys. These are surely by the same architect and, like Reid's house, may also be designs from Russell's office.

The history of inappropriate incursions into traditionally African American neighborhoods in Richmond has been widespread throughout the years and hardly any of these areas have escaped wholesale demolition from highways, urban renewal, industrial development or other destructive schemes that are seldom visited on white neighborhoods. Despite its handsome appearance and reputation as one of Richmond's premier African American neighborhoods, Frederick Douglass Court was also besieged at various periods in its history. In its edition of February 23, 1955, the title of the lead editorial of the *Richmond News Leader* thundered, "A Rezoning Move to Be Defeated." The story, which ran with photographs of houses in Frederick Douglass Court and a map of the area, urged the denial of a rezoning request to create a seventy-one-acre industrial area adjacent to the African American subdivision.[33]

The editorial lists four reasons why Richmond City Council should deny this attempt to create an industrial park filled with "coal and coke storage, contractors' plants and storage yards, fruit and food preserving and canning, paper box manufacturing,"[34] among other things, in an otherwise residential neighborhood. The first reason cited recognized Frederick Douglass Court and its architectural and social position in the city:

The first of these reasons—and it ought to be sufficient in itself—is simple fair play. Douglass Court, which lies to the south of the area sought, is the finest Negro neighborhood in Richmond. Representative houses in this well-to-do colored community are pictured above. If Council ever were offered a scheme to extend an industrial zone so as to ruin comparable white property, the scheme would be rejected instantly.[35]

The editorial also cited the inappropriateness of industry in the area, surrounded as it was by VUU on one side and what was then known as the Crippled Children's Hospital (today's Children's Hospital) on another. The third reason was the rather underhanded methods used by the developer in the acquisition of the property. The fourth reason the newspaper cited for denying the rezoning application was particularly interesting and indicative of this era of Richmond's history, with white flight to the suburbs changing Richmond's demographics. This reason also reflects the racism that was still very much inherent in the American South in the 1950s, and an uncomfortable attempt by Richmond to accommodate change in its racial composition:

For a fourth, impelling reason, Council has only to look at the changing population pattern we discussed editorially last week. Within the present Richmond city limits, Negro births now outnumber white births. It is of the keenest importance that land suitable for extension of well-defined Negro neighborhoods be reserved for residential use where possible. We do not need to discuss the social problems, the frictions and tensions that are created as a bulging colored population spreads into neighborhoods formerly occupied by white families. The one best way to prevent these unhappy situations is to see to it, as best we can, that at least an opportunity is kept open for existing Negro neighborhoods to grow naturally into adjacent open land...The Negro citizens who have invested in the attractive and pleasant homes of Douglass Court have every right to have this reoccurring worry of rezoning put to rest once and for all.[36]

In this rare instance, city council agreed and the proposed incursion into an African American neighborhood was denied.

Despite the call by the Richmond newspaper for simple justice, the reasons this attack on the fabric of Frederick Douglass Court did not occur are more complex. Richmond, like so many other Southern cities, tried largely unsuccessfully to stem the growing tide of the civil rights movement by rationalizing, defusing or circumventing the issues. This was an era when racial discrimination was being tested in the stores and streets of cities such as Richmond. City governments tried to slow the trend by half measures, attempting to steer, as well as contain, the development of African American neighborhoods. The editorial on the subject in the *Richmond News Leader* also reflects this self-serving philosophy, couched in terms of fair play for the besieged blacks of Frederick Douglass Court. It is ironic that this black enclave may owe its existence to just such maneuverings by the white press and city council of the period.

Despite the opposition by the community to the industrial rezoning scheme and the urging of the *Richmond News Leader* to the neighborhood to give "Not another inch!,"[37] there was a serious invasion on the southern edge of the neighborhood in the 1950s. The advent of the Richmond–Petersburg Turnpike (today's Interstate 95) threatened Frederick Douglass Court, as it did many other African American neighborhoods. One resident of the community pointed toward the end of the street and a handsome brick home at 1320 Dubois Avenue and recalled, "Oh, they wanted to take that one on the end and run the highway right here. But we stopped them and made them move it over."[38]

On the opposite side of Interstate 95 there is a commercial area filled with large brick warehouses. Outrage by the residents of the black neighborhood forced the movement of the path of the highway some yards south, missing the last houses on Dubois Avenue by a matter of feet. The same alteration to the path of the Richmond–Petersburg Turnpike caused the demolition of the ends of the brick warehouses on the south side of the highway. "Go over there and look for the new brick," the resident advised, pointing toward the highway that now looms above Frederick Douglass Court.[39] As promised, the warehouses at 1400 Overbrook Road on the other side of the interstate opposite the neighborhood show evidence that the end of the building has been demolished at some point and the wall rebuilt. This is mute evidence of the path of the interstate having been shifted to the south and away from the neighborhood and another victory for the residents of Frederick Douglass Court.

The parcel to the west of Frederick Douglass Court was finally developed, but a buffer of trees today protects the neighborhood from the landscaped grounds of the Wyeth Corporation Pharmaceutical Research and Development Center on Sherwood Road. This is a much happier fate than the smoke-belching industrial sprawl proposed in the 1950s that would have done so much damage to the neighborhood. It is hoped that the construction of the Wyeth complex will eliminate any further attempts to invade Frederick Douglass Court and reduce its few blocks.

The mixture of house styles seen today in the African American neighborhood at the corner of Brook and Overbrook Roads is not as coherent as the original developers intended. Instead of a community architecturally composed of three prescribed types of houses, the subdivision evolved slowly and organically, taking on new architectural types as the decades passed. To the earliest model homes were added substantial brick Colonial revival houses and Tudor-style houses in the 1920s and '30s. The postwar housing boom brought small ranch houses in the late 1940s and Spotswood Robinson's quintessential 1950s house.

Today, new infill helps complete the vision of a modern neighborhood of the type that the founders imagined more than seventy years ago: an enclave handy to the attractions and resources of the city but removed from the urban concentration felt closer to the core of Richmond. Renovation has also come to the area, and some of the oldest model homes are again resplendent. Despite the variety of architectural shapes and styles, Frederick Douglass Court remains unique in the Richmond cityscape as a suburban streetcar neighborhood founded by, built for, often designed by and well defended by the city's African American citizens.

7

Highways and Expressways
Navy Hill

"All of our history, traditions, good times and bad times were destroyed."
—*A former Navy Hill resident*

Over the last fifty years the city of Richmond has seen the impact of highways and expressways that slash across the urban grid. The sacrifice of entire city blocks, one after another, is the legacy of the rise of the automobile in American culture. It also represents the accommodation of suburban dwellers who demanded increased access to downtown employment. For one downtown neighborhood, Navy Hill, it meant the elimination of its homes and streets as well as its topography.

The neighborhoods targeted for wholesale clearance, either as part of "slum removal" or as highway construction, were typically poor and typically black. In preparation for the demolition of areas of the African American community in the early 1950s, a Richmond newspaper described a scientific approach in selecting properties:

> [D]etailed studies will be made of city records to determine areas of tax delinquency, lowest assessment and revenue production, areas where normal growth is impeded by slum conditions, and finally those slum areas most attractive to private developers.[1]

During these campaigns of "modernity" and "progress," the city's loss of many homes, stores, businesses and churches that had existed since the eighteenth and nineteenth centuries was staggering. The topography of modern Richmond has been worn down not only by the weathering of the seasons, but also by the hand of man. As an example, in 1860 Samuel Mordecai described a valley crossed by a bridge forty feet tall in the vicinity of Ninth and Clay Streets to "obtain access to the remote regions of Leigh Street."[2] Today this chasm has disappeared.

Navy Hill owed its name to just this type of steep landscape that ran along the northern edge of the city on the brink of the stream known as Bacon's Quarter Branch.[3] This area has been filled and bulldozed to the point that motorists skirting downtown on Interstate 95 are unaware they are driving in what was once a deep ravine. Into this valley projected a promontory, which was planned as a showplace of homes on either side of the street that ran down its spine. On the end of this point, a war memorial to the naval battles of the War of 1812 gave its name to the neighborhood, although it was never built. It was intended as a focal point, to be seen for miles around as it rose dramatically above the valley floor.[4]

As with the residents of nearby Jackson Ward, the population of Navy Hill moved from being a mixture of African Americans and German immigrants to almost entirely the home of black Richmonders. With additional residents and homes, the neighborhood grew outside the original design and moved into undeveloped blocks to the east and west. Although the core of Navy Hill was North Fourth and Fifth Streets, the modern street called Navy Hill Drive is on approximate alignment with North Sixth Street.

Although somewhat overshadowed by adjacent Jackson Ward, Navy Hill was more than just an annex to the larger neighborhood next door, with its own culture and even appearance. Mary Wingfield Scott traces this distinctive character to the Germans who originally settled the area, saying that "the Navy Hill part of 5th Street had a very definite character."[5] These German builders seem to have set the architectural tone for many of the older buildings that still existed as African American homes when Scott compiled *Old Richmond Neighborhoods*. Even a hundred years after being constructed, many of these houses maintained a different character from those only several blocks away in Jackson Ward. Scott noted that, "beginning about 1905, colored people moved south on 4th and 5th. For the most part, the houses north of Leigh are well adapted to their use and are better kept up than those in most parts of Jackson Ward."[6] The distinctive character of Navy Hill, created by Germans and maintained by African American Richmonders, existed until the destruction of the area in the 1960s.

An important component of Navy Hill was its city school. "The new schoolhouses—one on 6th Street, Navy Hill, the other on Nicholson Street, Fulton—are now nearly finished, and will be ready for occupation by April," City Engineer Wilfred Cutshaw noted in his annual report in 1892.[7] Cutshaw's office (which oversaw construction of almost all municipal projects) designed two very similar Italianate-style brick schools for Navy Hill and the vanished community of Fulton, called Nicholson Street School. The plans for the two schools were designed with generous windows and ventilation to reflect the latest in school design. Navy Hill School and Nicholson Street School must have been the pride of their respective communities.[8] Certainly the contrast with the facilities that preceded the city school on Navy Hill must have been vivid for black students and their parents.

The story of Navy Hill, its school and its definition as an African American community are more heavily rooted in the events following the Civil War than most other Richmond neighborhoods. Where the local school was the heart of Navy Hill, the origin of that first school building and its location began with the establishment of Union authority over the former Confederate capital in 1865. The provost marshal's offices were established as part of the military government that controlled Virginia after the Civil War and ensured that the rights of African Americans were respected through enforcement of the post-emancipation laws.

By the late 1860s the frame buildings on Broad Street that had housed the provost marshal had been moved north into Navy Hill at Sixth and Duvall Streets. By the end of the decade, these frame buildings were being utilized as schools for the education of African Americans. Navy Hill School was also the only public school in Richmond that employed black teachers.[9] It had the highest attendance rate among city schools, indicative of the strength of the surrounding community and the level of parental support. Scores at the school were the highest among the African American schools in Richmond and better than some white schools.[10]

Among these black children who attended Navy Hill during Reconstruction was John Mitchell Jr. Although perhaps not the typical pupil at Navy Hill, Mitchell nevertheless represented the caliber of student that the teachers there could produce. Significantly, one of Mitchell's teachers at Navy Hill and a personal inspiration was O.M. Steward, founder of Richmond's first black newspaper.[11]

In the 1870s, Navy Hill School was unique in Richmond education in that it was staffed entirely by African American teachers. A tradition of achievement survived in the neighborhood until the area was erased by highway construction a century later. Frank Leslie's Illustrated Newspaper, *July 21, 1883.*

Despite the poor physical condition of the surplus frame buildings that were Navy Hill School, the spirit of the facility was superb. Assignment to Navy Hill was considered of great importance since almost from its earliest days the school had boasted an all–African American faculty. Perhaps it was here, in the center of the Navy Hill neighborhood, where Maggie Walker first understood the linkage between racial pride and cooperation with economics and property, since these things were stressed in Navy Hill School.[12] Indeed, in comments penned thirty years after leaving the humble and dilapidated frame school, Walker wrote, "My eyes have filled with tears, as I have gone back over the past, full and crowded with events, as I have traced myself from a seat in Navy Hill's school to this present occasion."[13]

In 1891, as a Richmond city councilman, Mitchell successfully lobbied to replace the old crumbling Navy Hill buildings with a new brick school.[14] One of the two former provost marshal's buildings where Richmond's best African American children were taught was declared unsafe in 1892. Both were finally demolished to make way for the new facility, which opened the following year.[15] Located at 740 North Sixth Street, the new building dominated the skyline of Navy Hill. It was typical of city schools of the period, a seventeen-room, two-story building boasting large windows for good lighting and high ceilings that helped dissipate the summer heat of Richmond.[16] Compared to the crude, barracks-like buildings of the provost marshal, the 1893 Navy Hill School must have been regarded as the height of fashion and municipal education.[17]

There was a sense of pride in the tiny African American Navy Hill enclave, both in its high-achieving schoolchildren, their new brick schoolhouse and the neighborhood itself. Mary Wingfield Scott devotes an entire chapter in *Old Richmond Neighborhoods* to the architectural character and diversity of Navy Hill and Fourth and Fifth Streets.[18] Photographs in her book illustrate the various handsome hundred-year-old homes of what was an African American neighborhood. Many of these that date from the nineteenth century would today be considered architectural gems worthy of restoration. When she wrote about Navy Hill in 1950 before the path of the interstate highway through Richmond would decimate both Jackson Ward and Navy Hill, Scott was justifiably apprehensive about the future of the area and its people. Regarding Navy Hill's Fourth and Fifth Streets, Scott wrote:

While 5th is the more prosperous looking of the two, it is less suited to residences...4th, on the other hand, is a quiet, sleepy street that seems to be going nowhere. Both are beautifully shaded with large trees. It is sad to think how many of these trees and how many quaint though not handsome old houses will fall in the swath cut by the proposed Express Highway.[19]

Even with this prediction of damage to the community, Scott probably did not anticipate the complete destruction of the Navy Hill neighborhood. The black families that once called these tree-lined streets home were scattered, never to return. The dramatic valley that the Navy Hill School once stood beside has been filled, and Bacon's Quarter Branch runs somewhere deep underground. The arrival of Interstate

The historic neighborhood of Jackson Ward suffered a decapitating blow in the mid-1950s when Interstate 95 cut through the area and entire blocks of houses and businesses were displaced. *Courtesy Richmond Newspapers, Inc.*

95 meant entire blocks of Navy Hill were not only demolished, but the very ground that these homes stood upon was excavated and removed. The grid of the area has been erased and few traces remain to speak of Navy Hill with its sturdy old homes and shaded streets.

Navy Hill School stood directly in the path of the proposed highway and its destruction was assured, despite increasing demand on the facility over the years. In 1952 a much-needed cafeteria and gymnasium wing was put on the south side of Navy Hill School due to the demands of the local residents.[20] "We worked hard to get that building," recalled a former Navy Hill resident, looking at the obliterated site of the neighborhood school. "Before we had that, the children had to eat in the halls."[21] Despite the improvements made to it, the closing of the Navy Hill School occurred in September 1965. Its demise was hastened by the imminent construction of the Richmond–Petersburg Turnpike and the erasure of so many of the area's homes. The remaining student body was divided between Baker School and Carver School.[22]

The construction of the Richmond–Petersburg Turnpike in the 1950s and its architectural, social and emotional impact on Richmond's African American residents cannot be overestimated. The displacement of families, destruction of entire neighborhoods and impact on young and old alike must have been enormous. Not since the Civil War had such a large group of refugees been seen in the city, and these displaced black Richmonders had no chance of returning to their homes. The destruction of the built environment wrought by the construction of the highway was complete, irrevocable and final. In May 1957 the *Times-Dispatch* reported that:

> *Since January two years ago, about 1,900 Negro families have been evicted from their homes, mostly in slums north of Broad St., to make way for the Richmond–Petersburg Turnpike and other developments. In the next few months another 300 or more families will be ousted. These people, about one-tenth of the estimated 75,000 Negroes in Richmond, have generally found or will find new homes in two places—doubling up in existing Negro areas or moving into previously white areas.*[23]

The idea that the loss of neighborhoods, homes, schools and churches for any municipal project would be borne exclusively by one segment of the population is today repugnant. If any white people lost their homes or were otherwise inconvenienced by the highway construction, the *Times-Dispatch* does not note it. Instead, the newspaper describes how many of the displaced blacks would find homes among the 1,232 new subsidized housing units being opened in Richmond. When all the subsidized housing was complete, there would still be a thousand African American families who remained homeless. "This is the short-term picture." The same article continued, "By July 1958, if the Negro population were not to rise, the situation should be much better. But no one expects Negro population growth to stop."[24]

No mention was made of the loss predicted by Scott of the houses of Navy Hill by construction of the Richmond–Petersburg Turnpike. One by one the homes of the neighborhood disappeared. The school itself finally fell in 1965 after standing alone and empty amid the now vacant lots that had been Navy Hill. "All of our history, traditions, good times and bad times were destroyed," recalled one former resident of the old Richmond neighborhood.[25] Along with the obliteration of an entire African American neighborhood and the loss of blocks of handsome building stock, the tradition of education in this part of Richmond that reached back to the earliest days of emancipation had come to an end.

Even after the demolition of the school itself, the 1952 cafeteria addition to Navy Hill School was allowed to remain. This low utilitarian building stood just outside the highway fence in what became a featureless urban prairie north of the Richmond Coliseum. For many years the former cafeteria housed various public programs and agencies, finally becoming the home of the Richmond Children's Museum in 1980.[26] By 2000 that addition was also demolished.

For the sharp eyed, a few vestiges of this once-thriving African American neighborhood could be seen as late as 2005 and offered the barest hint of the tree-lined streets and handsome houses documented in *Old Richmond Neighborhoods.* On the corner of Navy Hill Drive and East Jackson Street, a tiny portion of what had been the masonry enclosure of a front yard had unaccountably been allowed to remain. An examination of the surface of the parking lot near this corner revealed the outline of foundations and basements barely sticking above the gravel. A cobblestone alley remained nearby and ran through a parking lot where backyards were once filled with the students of Navy Hill School. Today, the last traces of Navy Hill have been obliterated by the construction of the Virginia Biotechnology Research Park.

The site of the school itself was consumed by the on-ramp used by southbound traffic moving from Interstate 64 to Interstate 95. Scattered, however, in the parking lot beside the fence only feet from the highway are heavy granite lintels and sills, no doubt the last remaining fabric of Navy Hill School. Year after year, black students strode across these sturdy pieces of granite into their school, or leaned on them as they gazed over the rooftops of their neighborhood.

It is not hard to imagine that John Mitchell crossed one of these granite thresholds as he entered to inspect the new school in 1893, exploring the rooms with quiet satisfaction and approval and remembering the dilapidated Navy Hill School building he knew as a child. The lingering presence of these massive beams of granite hint at the strength that was once the school and the community it served.

A last poignant reminder of that neighborhood is hidden in the grass at the corner of Navy Hill Drive and East Duvall Street. A granite marker, much like a tombstone, reads:

> *Dedicated to the memories of our demised loved ones. July 17, 1993 Love and memories never die as days roll on and years pass by deep in our hearts memories are kept of the ones we loved and shall never forget. Donated by the Bob Curry Society, The Navy Hill Reunion and Friends Bob Curry President, B.H.W. Penick, Treasurer.*

The marker was placed on the occasion of a reunion of Navy Hill residents, many of whom came from out of state to revisit the altered landscape of their childhood.

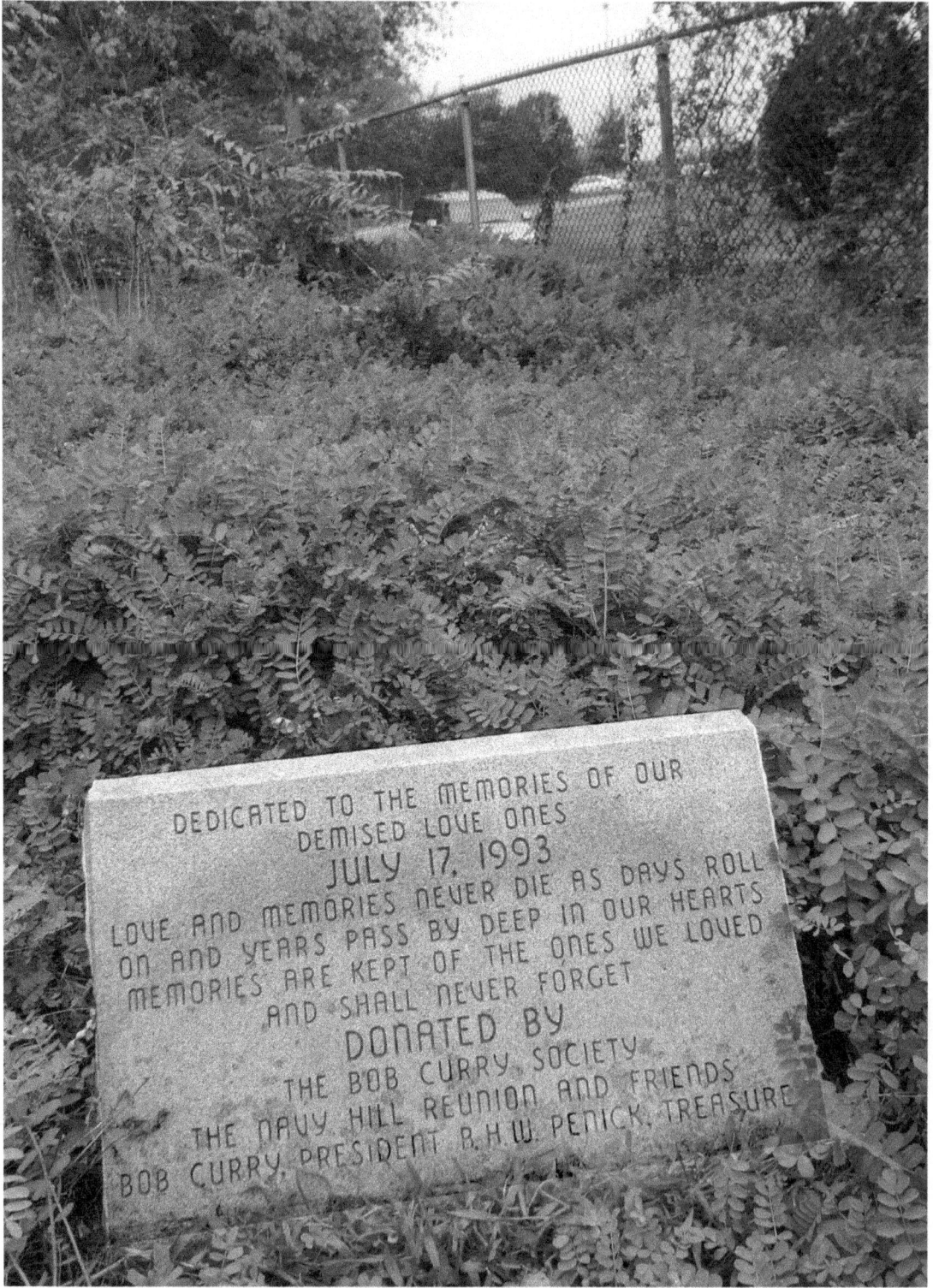

"This is the home where I received my early nurturing," recalled one former Navy Hill resident. "It was a unique composite neighborhood of families who cared about everyone else."[27]

Richmond has its vanished African American neighborhoods, but none so graphically or heart-rendingly recalled as with this tiny marker where Navy Hill stood. The memorial placed to recall the Navy Hill School and all the residents of this distinct community is a tombstone for a dead neighborhood.

One of the great losses, both architecturally and socially, to eastern Jackson Ward and Navy Hill was the dissolution of the congregation of the Fifth Street Baptist Church at 705 North Fifth Street. The church had suffered from the dismembering of Jackson Ward and the erasure of Navy Hill, and as a consequence of this loss the membership migrated to more suburban neighborhoods. The bitter feelings that developed from this conflict would eventually ensure the destruction of the building itself and lead to a major architectural loss in this part of the receding Jackson Ward neighborhood and the last architectural anchor to the east that once defined Navy Hill.

The establishment of Fifth Street Baptist Church dates back to 1880, the congregation being a daughter church whose members had originally worshipped at First African Baptist Church on Broad Street. This offshoot originally met in an Odd Fellows Hall on Franklin Street, near the city market.[28] Ironically, the building in Shockoe Valley was the scene of many slave auctions. The same walls that rang with praise once echoed the cries of separated families.[29]

Fifth Street Baptist Church utilized the historically tainted but still serviceable Odd Fellows Hall until 1886, when it acquired a Gothic-style church on Fifth Street from a German Lutheran congregation.[30] This was its home until the dedication of a new structure in 1926, whose wide columned and pedimented sanctuary stood on the same Fifth Street site. In an ironic echo of its earliest experience, the congregation again used a temporary public space while the new building was being prepared.[31]

The new church building on Fifth Street was designed and built by Davis Brothers, Architects and Builders. This Richmond firm was responsible for construction of a large percentage of the houses and churches in Richmond's Fan District, most of which, like Fifth Street Baptist's new sanctuary, the firm designed itself.[32] This handsome church displayed the pedimented front with recessed columns that was characteristic of so many African American Richmond churches, perhaps as an homage to the architecture of First African Baptist Church on Broad Street, from which so many of these congregations descended.

The church building on North Fifth Street served generations of Jackson Ward's black families, and the congregation at one point numbered two thousand persons. The decimation of the neighborhood by demolition and the division of Jackson Ward by the Richmond–Petersburg Turnpike (whose path narrowly missed the church) meant that by the mid-1970s the membership mostly lived in the Northside area of the city. In February 1975, the congregation voted to negotiate the purchase of the former Northside Baptist Church on Third Avenue in what a newspaper termed the "racially changing Highland Park" neighborhood.[33]

Of the 950-member congregation, the *Richmond News Leader* noted, 200 opposed the move to the Northside. As a commentary on the devastation to the Jackson Ward and Navy Hill communities wrought in the 1950s and '60s, only 35 members remained in the downtown area that once constituted the home of the entire congregation.[34] The proposal to move from Fifth Street immediately divided the congregation into two camps and their positions were intractable.

The majority congregation of Fifth Street Baptist Church went on to enjoy its new home in the Northside area as one of the first African American churches established there after the area became popular with Richmond's blacks. The diaspora of African Americans out of the shattered Jackson Ward and Navy Hill neighborhoods filled the pews at the new Third Avenue church. The splinter group that remained behind called itself the Baptist Church at Fifth and Jackson Streets, and occupied the old sanctuary until December 1977. After that date they, too, reluctantly moved from the building and began worshipping in their own church on Garland Avenue.[35]

The long story of the loss of this classical church building is not uncommon, and many other large and important structures in Jackson Ward and Navy Hill were destroyed in the years after World War II. What makes the demolition of the Fifth Street Baptist Church building so poignant is the acrimony that attended it. The sanctuary, instead of sheltering like-minded Richmonders sharing worship and praise, became a hotbed of division. The building was poisoned from within, and a 1980 article in the *Richmond Afro-American* newspaper shows it sitting sadly vacant, with a "for sale" sign nailed to the church's once-proud exterior.[36]

The 1926 Fifth Street Baptist Church was demolished in the early 1980s, but after the loss of the congregation this date becomes meaningless. The building was doomed at the point when its congregation fell apart. Presumably the deteriorating church building was demolished during the clearing of blocks of Jackson Ward in the area around the Richmond Coliseum and J. Sargeant Reynolds Community College projects in the early 1980s. The site is today buried beneath the buildings of the Virginia Biotechnology Research Park, and it is impossible to tell now where passions split a congregation and subsequently doomed a once-thriving downtown African American Richmond church building.

Unlike other threatened black neighborhoods, such as Fulton and Westwood, Navy Hill stood in the undisputed path of the city's growth. In addition to the interstate highway making inroads into the community, downtown Richmond was expanding. During the years that the area's domestic architecture was being dismantled, the medical complex of Virginia Commonwealth University was expanding into Navy Hill. The conflicting interests of preserving the neighborhood against university growth had to be carefully weighed. Unfortunately, the needs of the university, coupled with other kinds of commercial and city-generated ventures and the new highway, took precedence.

In the end, a pleasant tree-lined Richmond neighborhood gave way to a sterile zone of large-scale commercial development. For decades the city has attempted to reverse this tragic and outdated design, which was based on the rise of commuter culture. One of the goals of today's urban planners is to restore life to the streets of downtown. Regrettably, for those who grew up in Navy Hill and large areas of Jackson Ward, the loss of their homes can never be undone, and the world they knew and loved has disappeared forever.

8

Urban Destruction
as Urban Renewal
Fulton

"It was a dynamic, intellectual community."
—*A former Fulton resident*

In the eastern part of Richmond, the valley called Fulton is to the unknowing visitor an apparently blank slate of agricultural land that is only now being developed for homes. The broad valley north of Williamsburg Road is filled with grassy meadows, through whose soil pieces of brick and concrete occasionally protrude. Trees dot this meadow, some oddly in alignment, vaguely suggesting fencing or cultivation, but no real previous uses can be discerned. On the northern part of Orleans Street a grid of streets interrupts the grassland for a couple of blocks, then stops, suggesting the establishment of a planned town that never came to pass.

Actually, this appraisal of Fulton could not be further from the truth. Lots were for sale in what was known as the town of Fulton as early as 1853, when a reporter from the *Daily Richmond Times* speculated that the area would "soon become, we trust, a thriving little place."[1] In an interview in 1936, one resident who had lived in Fulton for almost eighty years described it as a well-established area of the city with its own stores and potteries, wharves on the James River, distilleries, a sugar refinery and a sail-maker's loft. These industries thrived in Fulton and Rocketts, on a grid of blocks originally laid out before the Civil War.[2]

Rocketts is the port area of Fulton along the James River, an area historic not only as the landing site for the early English settlers, but also the site of President Lincoln's arrival following the collapse of the Confederacy at the end of the Civil War. As in Navy Hill, the red brick city school was a structure that played a large role in the collective memory of blacks in Fulton and was a focus of pride and achievement. Fulton blacks were first educated in a small school building on Orleans Street, beginning in 1889. After several other locations were utilized for classes, the community welcomed the opening of a new school at 4410 Northampton Street in 1923. The school was named for D. Webster Davis, a highly respected black civic leader and teacher. Davis was described at the time of his death in 1913 as "an orator, pastor, author, businessman, musician, and poet," so naming the new school after this distinguished Richmonder was an appropriate honor.[3] The enrollment for that first school year was over 250, indicative of both the size of the thriving Fulton community and the need for the new Webster Davis School.[4]

View of Fulton, from Chimborazo Park, Richmond, Va.

P-63223

The community of Fulton, seen above on a period postcard, was a victim of urban renewal when it was razed in the 1960s. No vestiges of this once vibrant, early Richmond neighborhood remain. *Author's collection.*

Fulton was a part of Richmond that was then as densely populated as is the Fan District, a popular area in the city's West End. Much of the housing in the Fulton area resembled the same wood and frame row houses now commanding high prices in Richmond. Photographs of the neighborhood documenting its final days show the typical corbelled brickwork, Queen Anne–style towers and wood scrollwork so prized today in Jackson Ward. Block-long rows of brick townhouses lined the streets interspersed with plain, working-class frame houses of the type seen in Oregon Hill. If it still existed, Fulton would be highly desirable as a neighborhood handy to downtown and energized by development along the river. Instead, of the 850 homes of Fulton, the churches, schools, stores, small manufacturing facilities, alleyways and even the streets and drainage, nothing exists. Today, no trace remains of this extensive neighborhood of hundreds of buildings that once covered the two-hundred-acre site.

The story of Fulton is that of bureaucracy powered by the engine of urban renewal of the 1960s and 1970s. The destruction of Fulton began with a benevolent approach to the residents in the name of preservation, but concluded with the sanitizing power of the bulldozer as its principal tool.

By 1967, Fulton was termed by a Richmond newspaper "sick" and "shaggy."[5] While describing the area as the "birthplace of Richmond" and praising its interesting history, the *Times-Dispatch* said Fulton at the same time *seems destined to cease to exist as a predominantly residential neighborhood* [and is a place] *lacking social inhibitions, which are reflected in terms of illegitimacy and promiscuous behavior…For the years that have swept over Fulton Bottom have battered it into a state of virtual ruin. Age, neglect, abuse and the encroachment of industry have transformed Fulton Bottom into a slum, the worst in Richmond…Reports and statistics cannot sharply convey the dismal mood of a slum like Fulton Bottom. Only a visit to its streets and into its homes can reveal its bitterness and despair.*[6]

This bleak assessment, penned by investigators in the employ of the Richmond Redevelopment and Housing Authority (RRHA), an agency responsible for the local application of the urban renewal movement, amounted to a death sentence for the blocks of nineteenth-century homes, churches and stores of Fulton. A survey of Fulton residents indicated the need for a complete reengineering of the community. An observer of the decline and death of Fulton wrote of this survey and the reaction to it by neighborhood residents:

In 1967, the RRHA, with the help of city sanitarians, conducted a door-to-door survey as a preliminary to urban renewal. Fulton residents politely answered the questions the surveyors asked. Still, they were apprehensive. To them, urban renewal…focused all the ineptitudes and prejudices inherent in the city on the objects they most dearly cherished—their houses.[7]

Relying on the RRHA findings, permission was obtained from city council to prepare a redevelopment plan that would result in the demolition of much of Fulton and its reuse as a commercial and industrial area.[8] Having embarked on the planning process for the neighborhood, the bureaucrats who administered the urban renewal process in Richmond were astonished to find that Fulton was not morally and spiritually bankrupt, but rather that this African American community was the vessel of a "robust community spirit." Poor it may have been, but "to the 2,939 persons who live there, Fulton Bottom is home—a place to protect, to preserve, and, if possible, to perfect. Impoverished, yes, but not unloved."[9] In 1988, long after the Fulton neighborhood she knew in her younger days had been ground to dust, a former resident recalled in an interview:

It's the same neighborhood that [the U.S. Navy's first black admiral] *Sam Gravely came from. When people say it was poor and make disparaging remarks about it, we don't understand that. It was a dynamic, intellectual community. Everybody subscribed to the* Afro, [Richmond's African American newspaper]. *We were voters. We had our own doctors. We had two shoe shops. We had two drugstores. There were so many things that made it such a vital, dynamic community…We never thought we were poor until we heard other people talk about it. People had their own homes. They had good jobs…My aunt says that for the number of people and the area, there were more African American professionals in that neighborhood than she felt were anywhere else in the city. My grandfather was one of the people who worked along with Maggie Walker in starting Consolidated Bank.*[10]

Despite the feelings for their neighborhood, the African American residents of Fulton were soon to experience firsthand the frenzied urban renewal movement of the period. A "renewal" plan of the area was published showing a master plan for the Fulton area with the notation, "If City Council approves, the RRHA may begin acquiring property in the area by 1970."[11]

Although there were parts of Fulton where the building stock was on the point of collapse, the majority of the property the RRHA was planning to demolish was not in a stereotypical "slum" filled with abandoned houses. The African American neighborhood of Fulton was more than a particular pocket of buildings—it was a community in every sense of the word. The *Times-Dispatch* noted:

> *Approximately forty per cent of the houses in the area are occupied by their owners, and many of these, in striking and refreshing contrast to the area's general shagginess, are sturdy structures that show signs of care. In many of these homes live families whose roots are deep in Fulton—people born and raised in the neighborhood and in the process of raising families there.*[12]

Among those whose Fulton roots ran deep was William O. Henderson, the chairman of the Fulton Ad Hoc Committee, a group formed in reaction to dissatisfaction with the RRHA's plans for the area. Born in Fulton in 1917, Henderson had lived in the neighborhood ever since. He lived on Denny Street in 1968 when the community formed the ad hoc committee.[13] Residents such as Henderson knew full well what surrender to the planners and administrators of the urban renewal agencies in Richmond would mean for Fulton: its annihilation. And he was passionately determined to fight that outcome. At a second mass meeting of the community group, Henderson said, "I pledge myself to you now, that as long as I have breath to breathe, those bulldozers will not come into Fulton."[14]

The ad hoc committee worked for over a year on an alternate plan for Fulton, a plan that would provide for more residential areas and less industrial zoning. The master plan had originally called for the reduction of residential areas of the community down to 50 acres, with 170 acres of this formerly densely occupied African American community to be demolished and given over to industrial uses. Under the ad hoc committee, residents successfully fought to have the balance between industry and community equally split at about 110 acres each.[15] As part of the compromises made at the time, a buffer was proposed between the residential streets of Fulton and the industry that had grown along the James River. "A band of commercial development, including small businesses, retail stores, and drive-ins...suggested roughly along the portion of Williamsburg Avenue where there are many such businesses now," was planned as one of these transitional areas separating the homes of Fulton from the busy warehouses and factories on the southern edge of the neighborhood.[16]

At the time, the interaction between the African American residents of Fulton and the RRHA was described as a model of cooperation. Frederic A. Fay, executive director of the authority, described this interaction as "a new look" in urban renewal, one involving community participation. "And this is good, for it develops a sense of community pride."[17] Fay also noted that any action in the residential area of Fulton would include rehabilitation of houses that could be saved, and that some residents would be entitled to federal grants to help them finance these rehabilitation projects.[18] Under this scenario, a large number of the handsome row houses and homes in Fulton would not only be preserved from demolition, but residents would also receive funding to renovate these blocks and blocks of houses. Potentially, Fulton could have had the same charm and character that is today cherished in the Fan District, Jackson Ward and Oregon Hill. With proper planning and funding, Fulton could have been a remarkable and popular enclave of small, winding streets, charming row houses, thriving churches and neighborhood stores.

Former City Councilman (and later State Senator) Henry L. Marsh III, who represented the residents of the neighborhood at city council during this period, recalled the fight to save residential Fulton. His recollection confirms that Fulton residents themselves were the ones who worked to save their community and Marsh himself had to stand aside in the face of this powerful force:

> In contrast to that stark poverty, part of Fulton had very proud, neighborhood-oriented, community-minded citizens, and they loved Fulton and would do anything to help their community. The spirit and determination of the people not to have their community destroyed was as strong as any exhibited by any community in this city in recent memory.[19]

Yet for all this determination among the residents of Fulton, the area had begun a slide into what proved to be its ruin. In 1971, Scott C. Davis moved to Fulton as part of a two-year commitment to public service as a conscientious objector to the Vietnam War. He came to Richmond to work at the Bethlehem Center, a church-affiliated agency that assisted residents with government assistance programs. "I left Richmond in 1973 and went back to my hometown of Seattle but kept thinking about Fulton," recalled Davis in 1988. "Something did not add up. Millions of dollars had been spent to revitalize the neighborhood—yet it was destroyed."[20]

Davis returned to Fulton to interview the scattered former residents and to write an account of "the unmaking of a black community." His book, *The World of Patience Gromes: Making and Unmaking a Black Community*, follows the history and decline of Fulton, and its eventual destruction. Davis's chronicle of the decline of Fulton is an examination of the area and its residents and their relationship to their built environment. It also chronicles the slow and corrosive effects of the change that eventually undermined and overwhelmed what had been a solid neighborhood. Absentee landlords who refused to maintain buildings degraded the condition of rental property in Fulton. The arrival of heroin to the streets of Fulton, and all the urban ills that followed it, dissolved the bonds that once kept neighbors together. The bureaucratic engine of urban renewal that was as confident in its procedures as it was unthinking in its methods eventually assured the destruction of the neighborhood.

On top of all this, the James River flooded into Fulton in 1972, ruining homes along the southern edge of the neighborhood. "The flood took fifty families from Fulton," Davis wrote.

> *And even after the water subsided and the river flowed within its banks, the flood continued to drain this neighborhood in ways not apparent to the eye. The flood drained the will of Fulton's third generation to continue living here. In its wake dozens of elderly homeowners decided to take the $15,000 grants and move.*[21]

With the departure of this group of flood victims, the end of Fulton as a neighborhood was within sight.

Davis's chronicle of the area, as seen through the eyes of his elderly African American host in Fulton, is the story of the slow erosion of the social sinews that bind a people to a community. His elegy for a people and a place that was dissolved and demolished includes an attempt to define the dynamic that makes a geographic area of a city a neighborhood and a group of buildings a home:

> *A kind of glue held Fulton together, made it more than a chance collection of wood and brick and people strewn about in the hollow by the river. After the flood the glue was weakened and began to lose hold. It would be only time now and the last stores would close, the last people would leave, the last houses would splinter before the bulldozers.*[22]

An official history of Richmond public schools recorded the last days of Fulton's Webster Davis School as the neighborhood deteriorated, noting that despite community opposition, the facility was "discontinued in 1973, due to the expense of maintaining a full staff with a low enrollment," and its students were transferred to nearby Robert Fulton School on Fulton Hill. Webster Davis School was among the most overt symbols of commitment to Fulton by the City of Richmond. Its maintenance and staffing meant that Fulton was a viable community with a future, and its loss was an unmistakable signal that the neighborhood was in terminal decline. Webster Davis School, once the pride of Fulton, was boarded up and declared surplus by the city in July 1974.[23]

Among the very last buildings left in Fulton were the two principal churches in the community, Rising Mt. Zion Church and Mt. Calvary Baptist Church. Standing above the flattened blocks of Fulton like beached ships, these structures watched as their congregations receded and the lights gradually went out in Fulton. In the end, they, like the people they ministered to, had to move. And like many of their congregants, one chose to move to the reconstituted Fulton of today, while the other church moved to another part of the city, far from its home of over a hundred years.

A church that was rebuilt and continues to serve a new population of Fulton is Mt. Calvary Baptist Church, now located at 4401 Hobbs Lane. Like its parent church, Rising Mt. Zion, Mt. Calvary had always been in Fulton, first meeting there in 1880. In 1912, the congregation built a new brick sanctuary at 717 Orleans Street, replacing a wooden chapel constructed in 1888.[24] On the grounds of the new facility on Hobbs Lane is a memorial that includes the cornerstone of the Gothic-style 1912 church. On the top of this monument is the broken bell from the steeple of that structure, an appropriate memorial that once rang through the streets of now-vanished Fulton.

The church that moved away from Fulton was Rising Mt. Zion Baptist Church at 800 Denny Street. This was a congregation that traced its history back to the earliest days of emancipation, having been founded shortly after the fall of Richmond in 1865. Since its inception, Rising Mt. Zion had been in Fulton in various rented buildings until 1893, when a Gothic brick church was constructed. In 1940, the interior of Rising Mt. Zion was described as "stained glass windows, gallery around three sides, choir loft at the back of the pulpit, ceiling paneled in cherry stained wood, cream colored walls, light oak furniture."[25]

In October 1977, the congregation of Rising Mt. Zion held a farewell service on the steps of their 108-year home and formed a motorcade of more than 250 cars to their new building at the corner of Hartman Street and Elkridge Lane in nearby Henrico County.[26] Although the congregation had moved, they hired one of the last residents of Fulton to watch over the building and ward off vandals who would have stripped it of its furnishings.[27] He was Spencer Armstead, then 27 years old, and his attempt to save a tiny portion of the architecture of Fulton became the last sad chapter in the story of the complete destruction of that African American neighborhood.

"Some black folks say you've got to go back to Africa to find your roots," Armstead told a newspaper reporter. "Anytime I want to feel a little roots, I just walk up the stairs into the room I was born in."[28] Armstead and his mother were the only remaining residents in a row of nine brick houses on Denny Street that were the last group of buildings in Fulton. Both he and his mother were born in the house. In 1971, the distinguished architectural historian Dell Upton examined the row of houses. Upton, who worked at the time with the Virginia Historic Landmarks Commission, found the row of buildings had great merit:

> These houses are distinguished not only by their individual merits and sturdy construction, but by the cumulative effect of the row...It was evident from my examination that the houses were sturdy buildings and not seriously deteriorated. Minimal rehabilitation could easily render them superior to any modern structures with which they might be replaced. For these reasons, it seems clear to us that the brick row in the 700 block Denny St. is eminently worthy of preservation and that no reasonable argument can be made for its condemnation and demolition.[29]

Armstead and a group of childhood friends had formed Together, Inc., in an attempt to save the former Rising Mt. Zion Church, the former Webster Davis School at 4410 Northampton Street, the row of houses on Denny Street and also a decrepit house at 819 Nicholson Street. The little Nicholson Street house was once the home of Vice Admiral Samuel L. Gravely, who grew up in Fulton. Armstead and his group believed that the house should be preserved, and more than a street winding through "a wasteland of vacant lots"[30] should commemorate Fulton's most famous son.

Indeed, Gravely was the kind of person who exemplified the spirit that Fulton once produced. Reared in the segregated society of the day, he joined the navy in 1942 during a time when African Americans rarely were assigned to more than lower ranking jobs either on ships or shore stations. Early in his career Gravely spent his spare time in study and determining ways that he could take advantage of every opportunity that came his way. During the early years of World War II he held a variety of low-level assignments largely reserved for blacks, but soon he educated himself sufficiently to receive a commission as an officer. The obstacles were still there however, as he was forbidden by navy protocol and tradition to enjoy the amenities of such things as the officers' club. Not one to be dissuaded, he spent his segregated leisure time completing correspondence courses. With the passage of time, Gravely steadily rose through the ranks, becoming the first African American to captain a navy combat ship and the navy's first black admiral. He ultimately became the commander of the Third Fleet. At the time of his retirement, he had seen thirty-eight years of active duty and had served in World War II and the Korean and Vietnam Wars.

A profile of Armstead described the earlier interaction between the Fulton community and the aims of the activist and his friends. "Roots do not have a place in an urban renewal

Longtime Fulton resident and community activist Spencer Armstead sits on a barricaded street in the ruins of his community. The house (in the distance to the right) was occupied by Armstead and his mother and was the last of the many row houses that lined the streets of Fulton. *Courtesy Richmond Newspapers, Inc.*

plan," said the *Times-Dispatch* article. "The plan, after all, was devised by other people with their own roots in the same community. They decided that the best thing to do was to tear the whole place down and start over." In the same article, Armstead countered with the observation that the residents who had acquiesced to the destruction of Fulton were older, and those who saw no future in the neighborhood. Speaking of himself and his friends, Armstead said, "We were the ones who would have been willing to come back into the community…The [area committee] just couldn't deal with us."[31] Armstead vowed, "They'll never get my house. I'll shoot them if they try to throw me out."[32] As his neighborhood disappeared in front of him, his preservation group disbanded in the face of the inevitable. Armstead was left battling the RRHA in court and, invariably, losing. He felt he had two choices: to take his case to federal court or have his house declared a historic landmark in order to save it.

By September 1980, all but the house Armstead and his mother lived in and the two abandoned homes on either side had been demolished two years before.[33] An article titled "Fulton: Populated More By a Spirit Than People" ran in the *Times-Dispatch* with a photograph of Armstead sitting with a disconsolate expression on one of the guardrail barriers that now blocked what had been a Fulton street. In the background, the only visible structure is his home in the distance: the remaining three row houses on Denny Street. The rest of the area is a perfectly flat and featureless urban prairie where the community of Fulton once stood. "But, man, anything would have been better than this," said Armstead, gesturing to the fields around his house. "This is just sad, man. It's just sad."[34]

Armstead and his mother, Marian, did win a reprieve the week after the *Times-Dispatch* article appeared. District Court Judge D. Dortch Warriner issued an emergency order to prevent demolition of Armstead's home on Denny Street.[35] This was after Armstead and his mother filed suit against the RRHA, contending that an environmental impact study was not filed on the demolition of Fulton, as had been done in another African American community, Randolph. The outcome would largely hinge on the findings of the Virginia Historic Landmarks Commission as to whether they were eligible for the National Register of Historic Places.[36]

Three weeks later, the Historic Landmarks Commission, by a five to four vote, decided that the Armsteads' house, the last home in Fulton and the last vestige of the hundreds of homes of African Americans that had made up the Fulton neighborhood, was not eligible for the National Register of Historic Places.[37] In a last ditch effort to stop the demolition of the Denny Street houses, Armstead's lawyer Sa'ad El-Amin presented an unusual plea from the review board of the Landmarks Commission.

The story of the Armsteads and their attempts to save their Fulton home is filled with ironies, but none so great as that in the comments of the Landmarks Commission heard before Judge Warriner on October 24, 1980. The *Times-Dispatch* reported:

> *"The indiscriminate demolition of an entire historic neighborhood is tragic," the board said in urging the RRHA not to knock down the three architecturally significant houses…their demolition will deny to future residents of Richmond this tangible reminder of a portion of its 19th century heritage.*[38]

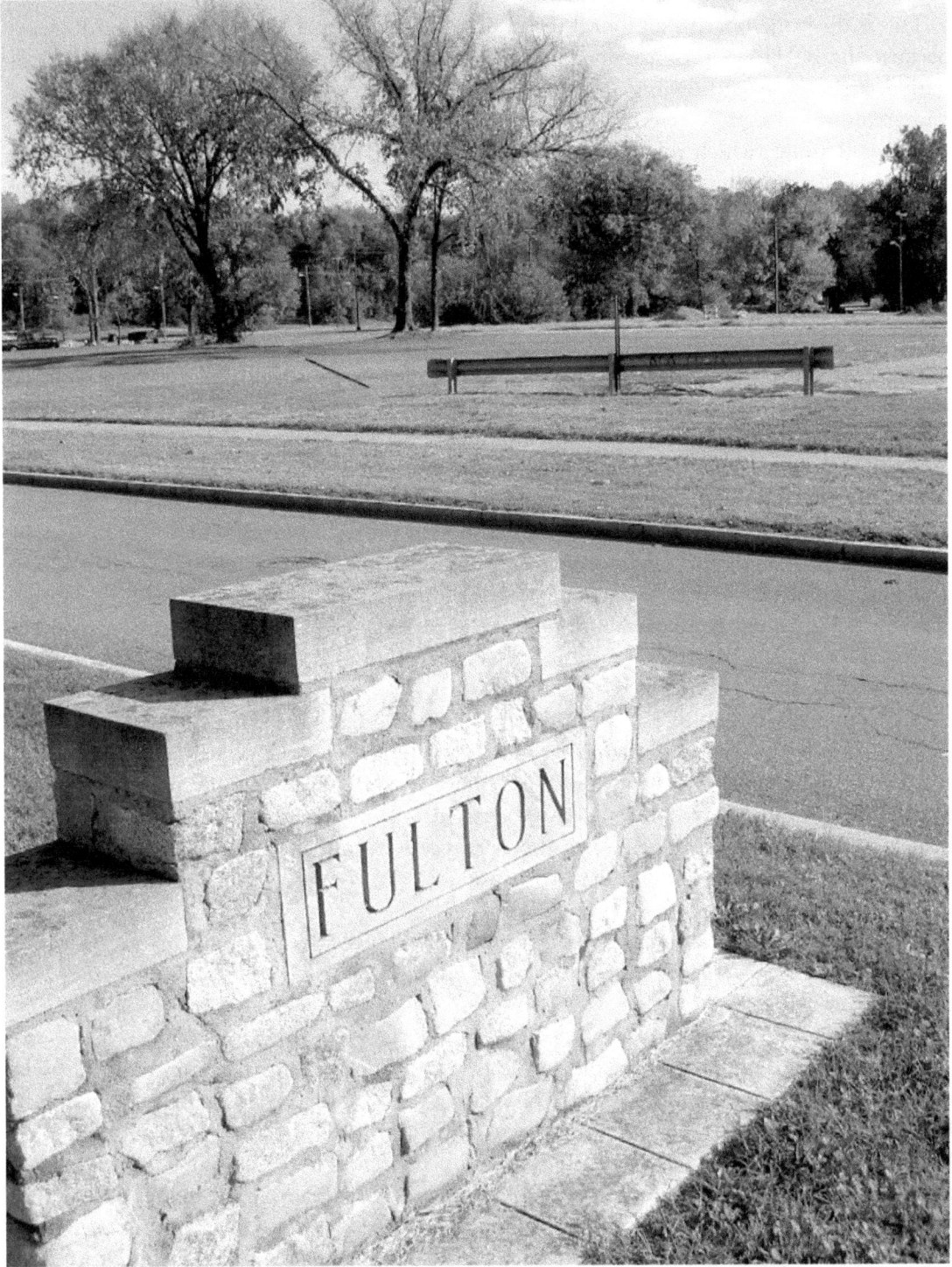

The marker placed at the entrance to the modern Fulton neighborhood of Richmond. In the background, a grid of abandoned streets still marks the site of the extensive African American neighborhood that once stood here. *Photo by author.*

This is the same board that found the houses were not suitable for the National Register because the RRHA, "in destroying the historic fabric of Fulton, violated the integrity of setting, association and feeling [that] once gave these houses so much of their historical and architectural significance."[39] The result was that the houses could not be placed on the National Register (which might have made their demolition more difficult) for the reason that all the surrounding neighborhood had been destroyed. Armstead's reaction to this circular logic was not recorded, other than his remark that city officials "just don't seem to be in with...the trend toward rehabilitation."[40]

On the other hand, Judge Warriner made no secret of his outrage about the demolition of 676 buildings in Fulton. "There was a community. There isn't one anymore," the judge told the RRHA's community development director, Robert S. Everton. "[Fulton residents] were afraid you were going to destroy [Fulton] and they were right." Everton countered that the renewal project was actually requested by the residents. "I would suggest that anyone not ask you to do favors for them," Judge Warriner responded. "They might end up—pffft—gone."[41] Warriner's valediction summed up the fate of Fulton.

Demolition continued, with the two surviving churches and Webster Davis School all falling before the bulldozer. Armstead and his mother moved away and the house they knew as home is also long gone, despite their efforts to save even that small part of their block. Today, the area he knew is unrecognizable, filled with ranch houses and tri-level homes, a dated design lifted from a suburban past. Woodbridge Village, a 250-unit apartment complex, was erected in the eastern end of Fulton Bottom in the late 1970s and a public housing complex was added to the area in 1980.

That same year an editorial ran in the *Richmond Afro-American* asking, "What Became of Fulton?"[42] The newspaper observed in hindsight, "Had many of the houses in the area survived to the present day, they would likely have become targets for the preservation and renovation movement sweeping the city today." Although this observation was too late to bring to the public attention to save the neighborhood and its hundreds of houses, the editors were able to assess the future of the area:

> *When the new Fulton emerges from the ruins, a whole different community will emerge. But Richmond will be the poorer for not having built that community on the foundation of the rich heritage of Fulton.*

The fabric of Fulton was completely destroyed yet the extensive community that was once there can be sensed, but not seen. The names of some of the streets in modern Fulton hint at a former incarnation of this part of the city: "Old Nicholson Street" and "Old Denny Street," without any indication of what once existed there. A granite marker placed at the intersection of Admiral Gravely Boulevard and Williamsburg Road states simply "FULTON." For those who once knew Fulton, the stone does not convey a welcome, but is a stark memorial to this vanished African American community.

Apart from the social implications of the loss of Fulton, the erasure of the architecture was significant. Nineteenth-century America witnessed the rise of many architectural styles, a number of which were reflected in the structures in Fulton. To be sure, the neighborhood never reflected the grand styles found in other parts of the city; however, it did typify the architectural styles and tastes of the day as they related to the working class. These kinds of neighborhoods are often the first to be razed in many of America's cities, and the reason is simple: they are almost always in areas that were the first to be developed and later deemed obsolete and encroached upon by commercial development. As businesses grew in the city, progress valued expanding commercial ventures over the retention of often modest residences. Such was the case with Fulton.

9

A Community Saved
Westwood

"Our forebears came from a very special situation."
—A Westwood resident

The story of Westwood is one of isolation, where this island of African Americans conducted their lives in a small village on the banks of Jordan's Branch. Theirs was a coherent and self-sufficient existence in what was then the country west of Richmond, and according to many of the older residents, it was a pleasant existence. Although Westwood was a world apart, it appears to have been rich with a sense of community. When asked about the Westwood of her youth in October 2003, one older resident, Jean Curtis, recalled:

> *Oh Lord, yes. And it was a feeling I'll never get again. Because the church and the community was one. Everybody who lived in here went to that church, and if anybody got sick, you know, people would come to your home and bring you things. We had hogs and hog killing time. My grandfather when he cut up the hogs always had a piece of meat for this one and a little piece of meat for that one. It was very nice up in here…But I think it was a good neighborhood. It was nice. You won't find that anywhere, I think. Most places now, people come from different places of the world, they just don't get that lovey-dovey anymore, and we all came, our forbearers came from a very special situation, you know. And they just, like, came together.*

In contrast to the fate of the Fulton and Navy Hill communities, Westwood, a small neighborhood in Richmond's West End, triumphed over the bulldozer. The destruction of this small, unique neighborhood would not have resulted in the loss of significant architecture because its built environment was modest and unimposing from the outset. However, unlike black neighborhoods in the central city, Westwood was embedded in a white residential suburb. As such, it developed a self-sufficiency that allowed it to flourish independent of its surroundings.

The most fundamental reason for development of distinctively African American neighborhoods outside of Richmond was that after emancipation free blacks were at liberty to move and seek work.[1] Originally, the policy of hiring out slaves in the antebellum period helped disperse the African American population into outlying neighborhoods and away from the urban "quarters" located behind many of Richmond's fine townhouses. Space did not allow the entire staff to stay on the premises and hired slaves were given an allowance to arrange their own accommodations. After the Civil War, Richmond experienced a migration of black workers away from the city, where, for instance, domestic workers settled in proximity to their white employers in places such as Washington Park.[2] On the other hand, farm workers from nearby King William and Hanover Counties moved to neighborhoods such as Providence Park to be closer to opportunities for employment in the city.[3]

Henrico's Zion Town and Richmond's Westwood are settlements that followed another pattern. Both were established after the Civil War by former slaves. In 1874 the first church in Westwood, a log structure, was built "by both men and women," a church history proudly recalls.[4] This was soon followed by a frame church building on the same site, a rise then overlooking the little valley that is today defined by Willow Lawn Drive. The church was typical of small, rural African American churches that dot the American South. Baptisms were held in nearby Jordan's Branch, a stream that abuts the Westwood neighborhood.[5]

Research cannot determine who laid out the streets and lots that make up the modern neighborhood of Westwood, but the history of the neighborhood itself and that of its church are largely one and the same. In 1876 land was transferred to the church "for the benefit use & disposal only of the members of the congregation known as the Westwood Colored Baptist Church."[6] This area was part of the property later divided into the small lots of the Westwood community. The church that still stands on the corner of Glenburnie and Lincoln Avenues gave rise to the neighborhood as it served as the emotional and spiritual heart of this African American community.[7]

The homes that sprang up around the Westwood Baptist Church were small frame structures and were typically built by members of the community. Although many homes were built immediately after World War II, several examples of the older houses still stand, primarily along Stokes Street and Marian Lane. The house at the corner of Parrish Street and Marian Lane is representative of the small, frame house with front porch and touches of Victorian-style decoration that the founders of the Westwood neighborhood built around 1900. These frame bungalows sheltered generations of Westwood residents who lived quietly in their self-contained enclave on Patterson Avenue.

Westwood had its own store and school. Because Westwood was such a small community and so isolated from the rest of the city, even blacks in other parts of Richmond did not believe in its existence.[8] It was a common perception that blacks worked in the West End but did not live there.

Interestingly, Westwood Baptist Church regards itself as a sister church to another small African American enclave off Broad Street, near its intersection with Glenside Drive in Henrico County. Known as Burrell Town, this area grew up around Pilgrim Journey Baptist Church.[9] Much of this neighborhood along Basie Road has vanished and the earlier building stock that would give an idea of the origin of the neighborhood has also disappeared. On

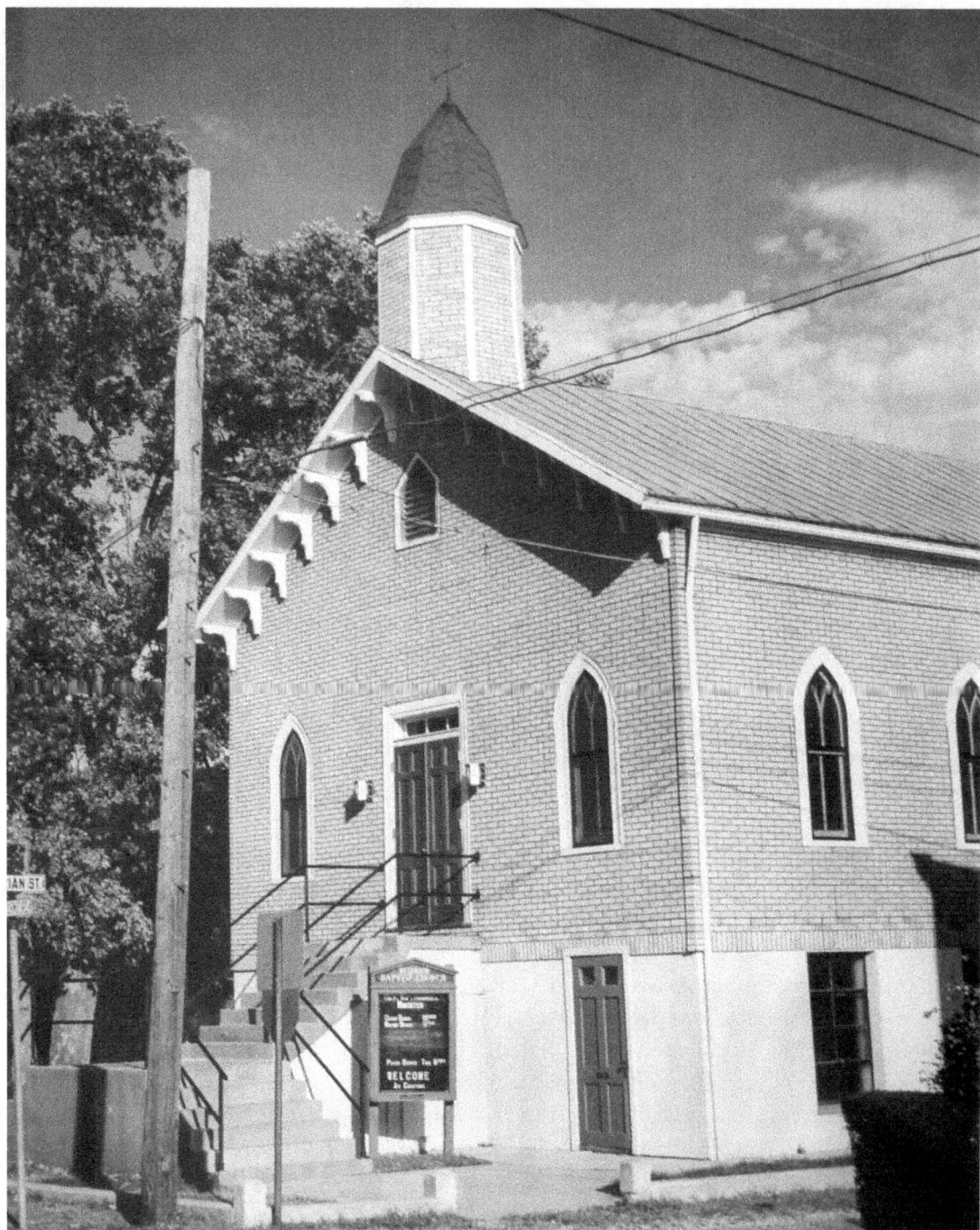

Westwood Baptist Church, organized in 1874, as it appeared in the 1950s. In the 1970s, the church was expanded and this building was encapsulated in the new structure. *Courtesy Kathleen Valentine.*

The current Westwood Baptist Church was built to incorporate the original church building. Behind the church is a cemetery whose tombstones were unfortunately removed decades ago.

May Day, Pilgrim Journey Baptist Church and Westwood Baptist Church still have a joint Sunday school service and celebrate their shared heritage.[10]

A small, two-room schoolhouse (now demolished) stood on the site of what is currently the community playground in Westwood. It served the community for many years. The neighborhood was annexed by the city in 1942 and the little frame schoolhouse continued to be used by the children of Westwood for six more years. A history of the Richmond Public Schools notes an enrollment in this tiny facility as thirty-five for the school year of 1943–44 and forty-one students in 1947–48. In 1948 it was closed, and Westwood students traveled by bus to Carver School.[11] Carver Elementary School is approximately five miles away and would have involved a bus ride of at least twenty minutes, while Westhampton School for whites was only two blocks from Westwood and within sight of the African American neighborhood.

The issue of segregated schools and bussing black children was only one of several problems visited on residents of the collection of bungalows that clustered around the Westwood neighborhood church. The story of the assaults against this neighborhood, the denial of city services and the repeated attempts to obliterate the entire enclave is worth recounting. It serves as a reminder of the conditions under which many Richmond blacks lived prior to the civil rights movement of the 1960s and 1970s. The story also speaks volumes about the sense of community enjoyed by this area, and the deep roots of Westwood that tied together the people, their homes and their churches.

Writing in *Race, Class, and Power in the Building of Richmond, 1870–1920,* Steven J. Hoffman describes a pattern of withholding essential city services such as water and sewer to African American neighborhoods as an obvious trend not only in Richmond, but in cities across the country as well. Hoffman wrote:

> *Enough evidence exists to suggest that the infrastructure needs of Richmond's African American and working class white populations were a lower priority than the city's upper and middle-class whites…Discrimination on the basis of race is readily apparent in the expansion of Richmond's infrastructure into the different neighborhoods of the city.*[12]

This tactic was never as blatant as the situation in Westwood. Nor was this form of discrimination more obviously used as a tool to attempt the destruction of an entire community, including the homes of the residents and even the streets on which they lived.

In 1945, the two hundred residents of Westwood were forced to draw water from one public hydrant on the corner of what is now Willow Lawn Drive and Patterson Avenue. The wells that had served some residents were condemned at the time of annexation. Ironically, taxes were raised at the same time the community was brought into the city of Richmond.[13] Residents of the white neighborhood to the south between Patterson Avenue and Cary Street began a campaign of pointing to Westwood and its inadequate facilities as the possible source of an outbreak of typhoid fever and they whipped up hysteria about their black neighbors to a fevered pitch. "Health Menace at Westwood," said a Richmond newspaper, noting:

> *The Board of Aldermen has rejected without comment the request of the Health Director that sanitary facilities be extended immediately to the Westwood settlement which is adjacent to residential developments in the homes of which many of the Westwood Negroes are employed.*[14]

Despite the Richmond health director stressing the need for clean water and sewer services, the measure was denied by the board of aldermen. Members felt that providing city water and sewer would "be followed by enlargement of the Negro settlement,"[15] a prospect at the time intolerable to the aldermen.

In addition to denying blacks the sanitary privileges that neighboring whites enjoyed, another measure was proposed in 1945 to demolish the neighborhood to build a park. The common council had on a previous occasion denied a motion to turn Westwood and the area surrounding it into a city park. The 1945 proposal, the subject of public hearings in which "Westwood residents appeared en masse,"[16] was dropped. However, this idea was revived a year later. The 1946 proposal would allow residents to live in the homes that their forefathers had established in Westwood to "live their lives out, but their children would have to move after their parents died."[17] The Westwood Baptist Church would be left standing as long as it was used by its parishioners, and a wall would be placed around the cemetery. Several West End community associations went on record as being in favor of the park, contending that there was a need for it in the area and its establishment "would result in the greatest good

This bungalow is typical of the early architecture of Westwood, a small, self-sufficient community in Richmond's West End founded by former slaves from the nearby Patterson plantation.

This exceptionally steep flight of stairs is indicative of the modest interiors of many houses in the Westwood area.

for the greatest number." This observation was made during a time when ample green space existed in this part of the West End.

This transparent attempt to destroy the neighborhood was opposed violently by the residents of Westwood, led by their pastor, the Reverend Alfred Waller. They were joined by several white citizens who lived nearby on the grounds that the park proposal was unfair and clearly "aimed primarily at driving the Negroes out of Westwood."[18] The spokesman for whites who supported the Westwood residents was Walter Craigie, head of the Richmond Community Council. Craigie also stated that he spoke for a "group of right-minded citizens"[19] who opposed this injustice. Craigie's was among the opposing voices again in 1947. By then the issue of city water and sewer had still not been resolved. The *Richmond News Leader* criticized the lack of progress on the issue with an editorial on the subject after publishing photographs of conditions in Westwood:

> We had to acquaint fair-minded Richmonders with the intolerable and shameful hardship imposed on residents of the old Negro village, Westwood. With illustrations and plain words we exposed a condition we know Richmond will not countenance—the fact that 53 of the 65 Negro households in that settlement have to get their drinking water from a single hydrant, which is as far as six blocks from some of their homes. Much as we dislike ever to have to use a word that indicts our society, where it is most sensitive, we must ask, is this fair play? Nobody can so regard it...Richmond will stand ashamed in the eyes of all men if she permits these conditions to exist.[20]

Public opinion appeared to support the city's position of denying basic public services. Again, the proposal for a park was introduced, provoking a heated public meeting (apparently of only area white residents) at nearby Westhampton School. The white subdivisions in the area such as the Colonial Place Association, the Monument Avenue Crest Association and Hampton Gardens Civic Association all sent representatives who spoke in favor of razing Westwood.[21] The Glenburnie Civic Association, representing the white residents in the area immediately to the south of Westwood, was led by an attorney named L. Gleason Gianniny, who stated the civic association would agree to "letting the present owners of houses in Westwood Village remain there for the rest of their lives."[22] At the same time the Glenburnie Civic Association endorsed running the necessary sewer and water lines to service what would be a dwindling and dying community. Dismissing the claim that the residents would have nowhere to go after being turned out of their homes, Gianniny insisted, "There are hundreds of places for them to go," and suggested they be transplanted to the areas south of Cary Street and east of Meadow Street.[23]

Craigie rose to speak on behalf of Westwood, saying that he represented not only concerned citizens who were opposed to the destruction of the neighborhood, terming the effort to demolish their homes "racial, pure and simple." Craigie stated that "it was a question of Christianity or no Christianity," a remark that was greeted with a mixture of cheers and boos. Craigie, who said he knew many of the Westwood residents by name, earnestly described them as "a helpless minority." He described them as "lying in their beds, trembling" with the thought of the forces gathered against them who would take away their homes, their community, their church and the very cemetery where their ancestors were buried. This remark brought considerable laughter, to which Craigie sharply replied, "This is no laughing matter." Craigie then handed Gianniny a proposal to extend the city sewer and water services, but the attorney ignored the document.[24]

Typical of the racial prejudice of the time, whites such as Craigie who expressed sympathy with African Americans, or hired them, were often described as "nigger lovers." This label was used to thwart the efforts of those who would help blacks and to shame whites who tried to lessen the blow of the whip of racial hatred. The response of the attorney hired by the Glenburnie Civic Association is reminiscent of this tactic, as reported by a Richmond newspaper:

> When Mr. Craigie had finished, Mr. Gianniny said that if Mr. Craigie was so intimately acquainted with the Westwood residents and liked them so well, "Let's move them all out on Cary Street Road [where Craigie lives]."[25]

The meeting at Westhampton School apparently yielded no consensus, and the eleven Richmond council members present left before Craigie spoke. Several days later, however, the *Times-Dispatch* printed as its lead editorial a statement titled "Westwood—Touchstone for Richmond." The appearance of the editorial in the principal newspaper of the former capital of the Confederacy, a city roiled for decades by issues of race and soon to enter the bitterly divisive decade of the 1950s, shocked many:

> The issue in the Westwood matter remains just what it was before some 200 citizens met in Westhampton High School on Friday night to discuss its pros and cons. That issue is whether Richmond's people, and their representatives in Council, are going to provide water and sewerage for 65 hard-working, law-abiding families who pay city taxes and are entitled to these facilities, or whether those citizens are to be denied such facilities because they are colored. This Westwood issue has come to be a touchstone, in a large way, of the civic attitudes and the sense of decency and justice which are controlling here. Seldom, if ever, have as many white Richmonders been as aroused over any issue involving interracial justice as have been aroused in the present instance. Hundreds who normally take no part in interracial discussions have considered this Westwood proposal almost a personal matter. They may question the wisdom of some things that are being done for the advancement of Negroes in the South and the nation, but they can see the utter unfairness of proposals that have been made for ousting the Westwood Negroes from their homes for the benefit of whites who moved into the area long after they did. Everybody knows, of course, that the "park" which is being advocated for the area has been held by the City Planning Commission to be unnecessary and undesirable.[26]

The editorial was applauded in letters from readers. One writer acknowledged the attempt to establish a city park on the site and level Westwood would never be attempted if the residents were white, and they would have been given the water and sewer service they so desperately needed without question. The same writer drew on the recent experience of World War II, very vivid in the minds of all Richmonders, when he commented:

> *Our contribution to a better world begins in our own community and that disregard for the wishes and rights of this colony would be a manifestation of the thing we have condemned in the despicable Nazi philosophy.*[27]

Other letters called for fairness for Westwood. The noted Episcopal Church historian, the Reverend George MacLaren Brydon, cited one of the qualities inherent in all neighborhoods as being a real and tangible asset that the people of Westwood would forever lose if they lost their homes:

> *The right of permanency of the community is a real property right and a vital element in the fixing of financial values. Will that value be taken into consideration if the city should destroy the Negro community?*[28]

With this final outcry, the fate of Westwood was settled. City council passed a resolution to extend water and sewer mains to the neighborhood on April 8, 1947, without further fanfare. But a proposal to create some streets and widen others was tabled. This was doubly fortunate because the proposal to widen the narrow streets of Westwood would have done serious damage to the houses of the area that are often sited close to the street on small lots.

Three weeks later, the Reverend Alfred Waller of Westwood Baptist Church announced that residents were ready to connect and the mandatory fees for connection would be paid. "If there is anyone who cannot afford the installation costs," Waller added, "the community will see to it that appropriate installations are properly financed."[29] Again, the residents of Westwood drew together to ensure that the services would be paid for and enjoyed by all.

One of the driving forces behind the resistance to the so-called "Westwood Park" plan was the presence of returned African American servicemen. Waller, in an interview for one of the many newspaper articles that appeared about Westwood and the assaults against it, cited the presence of forty men and women who had returned to the neighborhood from military service and who wanted to live in their home community, get married and build houses. This influence can be seen today in the number of postwar houses in Westwood, monuments to the triumph of the community over the forces that would have destroyed it. These houses built by returning black servicemen and servicewomen are today indistinguishable from similar housing constructed all over the city in the late 1940s.

The park plan appeared to fade from the public eye at this time, perhaps due to the resignation from office of one of its principal proponents, Alderman Frank S. Richeson.[30] "Westwood Park," the displacement of this community of African Americans and the destruction of their homes that was once described as "the greatest good for the greatest number," never came to pass.

Despite the challenges of remaining a coherent African American neighborhood, beset by discrimination and threatened by gradual demolition of its building stock, Westwood remains a unique Richmond neighborhood and a model of perseverance and pride. The relationship between their environment, the sense of community centered on the Baptist church and its building and the deep, fierce pride that drove the residents of Westwood to defend themselves in the 1940s did not die with the threat of obliteration posed by the park initiative.

In a footnote to the story of Westwood and the surrounding neighborhoods, the white Westhampton School was threatened with closure when three African American students applied to the school in 1958. A front-page headline in the July 1958 *Richmond News Leader* read: "3 Negroes Apply in Westhampton."[31] Today it seems absurd that an entire school with hundreds of students would close due to the registration of three children of a different race. This, however, was a period when many social questions such as the inequality of so-called "separate but equal" school systems were still being debated in Richmond and in Virginia in general.

Unfortunately, the *Richmond News Leader,* which had defended Westwood a decade earlier, did not choose to rise to its defense in 1958.

> *If these children and their parents now insist upon enrollment at Westhampton, and obtain a Federal court order compelling admission, the consequences will be bitter and the resentment great.*[32]

Citing the defense of the "helpless minority" of the 1940s as an example of good race relations and in an appeal for *status quo*, the editors of the *Richmond News Leader* plaintively asked:

> *Over a long period of years, the two races have lived amiably in Richmond on an old rule—the rule that one good turn deserves another. Is all that ancient history, too?*[33]

The issue of the racial integration of Richmond public schools would not be settled until the initiation of court-ordered bussing in the 1970s. Westwood students continued to be transported all the way to Carver Elementary School in the inner city, a journey that was "no real inconvenience" in the words of a Richmond newspaper in 1958.[34]

The perpetually vigilant Westwood community was powerless to defend itself against a unique affront: the theft of its name. A mile to the west of the community, at the corner of Monument and Libbie Avenues, a white subdivision was established that appropriated the pleasant-sounding name "Westwood." Today, a sign beside Monument Avenue at the corner of Monument and Bremo Road proudly proclaims "Westwood—Est. 1937." Typical of the times, the African American community on Patterson Avenue was ignored and considered in the 1930s a lesser entity, filled with people of a lesser value. Richmond now has two neighborhoods called "Westwood," but only the African American neighborhood can rightly and historically be called by that name.

A history of Westwood and its small bungalows and its strong Baptist church is incomplete without mentioning its best-known son, Arthur Ashe. In his autobiography, this world-famous African American sports figure wrote of his family connection with the neighborhood:

> My mother's side of the family was a little more fortunate than my father's. Her parents, Johnnie and Jimmie Cunningham (we called her "Big Mama," but her real name was Jimmie), came to Richmond from Oglethorpe, Georgia, and settled in Westwood, a small enclave of blacks on the western fringe of the city. Johnnie died in 1932, leaving Big Mama with ten children to bring up herself. With dignity, faith, and discipline, she did the best she could. In 1938 their daughter Mattie (nicknamed "Baby") and my father, Arthur Ashe, were married in Big Mama's living room and they even lived a long time with her.[35]

"Big Mama" Ashe's house at 903 Glenburnie, now neatly restored by its current owner, still stands; a small wooden bungalow with a west-facing front porch, just a short walk from Westwood Baptist Church. It is astonishing that the ten Cunningham children were raised in this little house and bears testimony to the perseverance typical of Westwood and its people. Ashe's memories of his Westwood grandmother are pleasant and powerful, and this celebrity furnishes in his autobiography a touching snapshot of one of the community's elder residents, a woman who probably lived among elderly ex-slaves who were there when Westwood was founded:

> I will never forget Big Mama. A deaconess at Westwood Baptist Church, she proudly wore her starched and immaculately white uniform with white shoes and a lacy handkerchief in her left breast pocket. I also remember the daily dollops she took of her beloved snuff, a kind of powdered tobacco, which she slipped under her bottom lip, and the empty Maxwell House Coffee can she kept close by to use as a spittoon. We all loved her. At her funeral in 1972, Uncle Rudi called out, "Goodbye Mama," as her casket went up the aisle. Then something in me simply burst open and I cried uncontrollably, as I had never cried before or since. Her grave is only about a hundred yards from my mother's grave in Woodland Cemetery in Richmond.[36]

House. Home. Community. Church. These are the threads that run throughout the Westwood neighborhood story and bind this unique place to its people. Although he was internationally famous and had traveled the world, Arthur Ashe cherished Westwood, and in his memory he returned to its dirt streets and little frame bungalows.

Westwood's history is singular because this is a story that was enacted on such a small stage, tucked away from the heavy traffic on nearby Patterson Avenue. As an architectural document, Westwood reflects the stages of development as it contains examples of early bungalows, postwar ranch houses and modern infill that have fortunately retained the scale and flavor of the earlier structures. Recent incursions along the Patterson Avenue borders have been eating away the community with construction of a post office, office park and a bank building. Despite this, Westwood thus far continues to prevail as an African American enclave with an important story to tell.[37]

There are, however, obviously troubling clouds on the horizon for this self-contained community. Since its eighteenth-century inception, Richmond, like almost every city in the country, has continued to grow. In the case of this city, the growth began and continues to move westward. Ten miles or so to the east, the area is sufficiently rural to remind one of what it must have looked like when the English arrived. To the west, however, the story is entirely different. The march westward began at the rim of Shockoe Hill, proceeding through community after community and often obliterating all before it. When the freed Patterson slaves first established Westwood, it was in a remote rural spot. Now being adjacent to a commercial area, rapid growth has already enveloped nearby places that little more than a generation ago were woodlands. Commercial development continues to chip away at the fragile borders of Westwood. Hopefully the community will persevere as it has for almost 150 years.

10

The City's Black Churches

"The Word of the Lord is my Defense and Bulwark."
—Sermon by the Reverend John Jasper

From the crude meetinghouses to the soaring Gothic churches, the story of the large and influential African American population and the structures its members built are an expression of their abiding faith. Among the earliest were First African Baptist Church (College and Broad Streets), Third Street Bethel African Methodist Episcopal Church and the First African Baptist Church, Manchester (later renamed First Baptist Church, south Richmond).

Perhaps the most striking example of this progression is the story of the Reverend John Jasper and his Sixth Mt. Zion Baptist Church. Beginning in a wooden shed in an abandoned Confederate horse stable on Brown's Island in the James River, the church now boasts a prominent building in Jackson Ward.

An important location for beginning a panoramic view of African American churches of Richmond is the corner of College and Broad Streets. This was the site of the original First Baptist Church, a large brick building that housed a biracial congregation and was constructed after the lifting of a ban against Baptist preaching. Built in 1802, it offered one of the largest spaces for meetings in the city and was used for political rallies and exhibitions.[1] After 1841, when white parishioners built a new church two blocks away at the corner of Broad and Twelfth Streets, they sold the older building to the African American segment of the congregation, which included both slaves and free blacks. In 1865, black Richmond crowded inside to hear Horace Greeley, the famous antislavery editor, speak on the future and promise of Reconstruction.[2]

The First African Baptist Church prospered and its congregation quickly outgrew the original building. An article in an 1874 edition of *Harper's Weekly* commented:

> The members of the First African Church, Richmond, Virginia, with true lack of American veneration for old things and old buildings, are preparing to demolish and rebuild their ancient house of worship, the oldest colored church in America, if not in the world.

An illustration accompanying the article shows a view of the rather plain interior of the church during a worship service, packed with its congregation that numbered almost four thousand. The *Harper's Weekly* article goes on to admit:

> *In spite of repeated additions to the church edifice, it is still much too small for its immense congregation, and the plans for the new building which is to rise upon its site are already in the hands of the builder.* [3]

The old church was demolished and in 1876 the new First African Baptist Church was completed. The design has been called a derivative of the nearby First Baptist Church constructed by the white congregation, and like the white church, featured a recessed entry porch flanked by columns. The term for this popular arrangement is *distyle in antis* and this architectural element was to become a strong thread that connected many Richmond Baptist churches, white and black alike.[4] Construction of the 1876 church is attributed to Richmond contractor T. Wiley Davis.[5] Although the new church did appear similar to that designed for the white congregation, the new building was undeniably commissioned by and built for African Americans.

The independence of First African Baptist—first from its parent congregation and then from the legally required oversight of a white minister—marked the true ascendancy of the

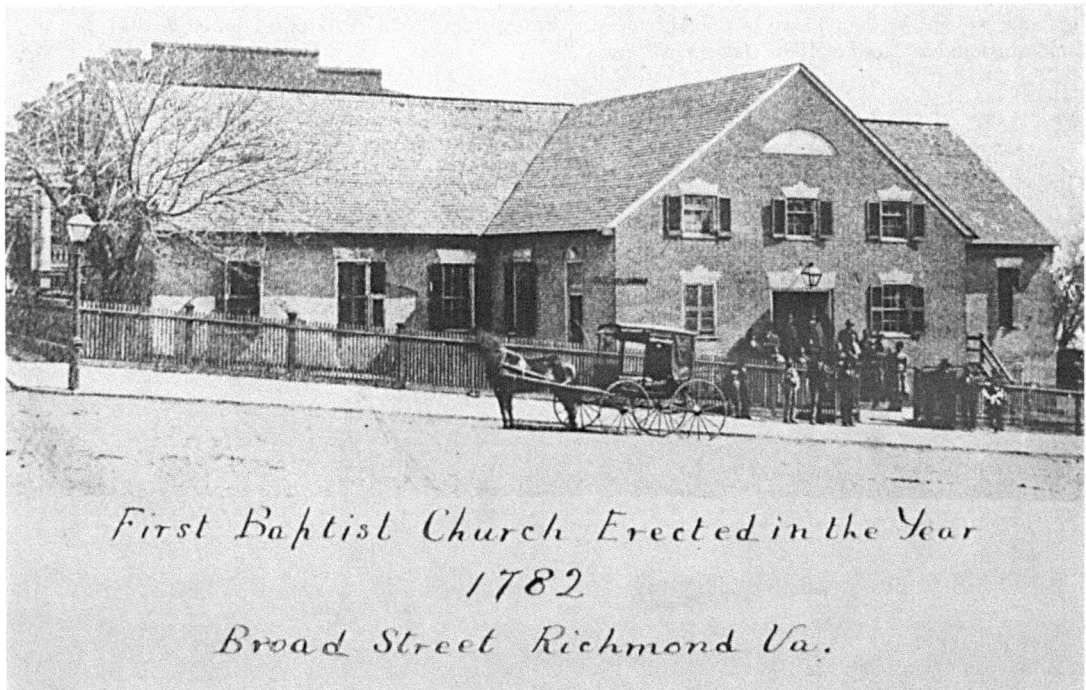

First Baptist Church Erected in the Year 1782 Broad Street Richmond Va.

Members of the original First African Baptist Church included both free and enslaved blacks. One of the oldest black churches in America, the structure was among the largest buildings in Richmond and was used for political rallies and exhibitions. *Courtesy Valentine Richmond History Center.*

The interior of the original First African Baptist Church as it appeared in *Harper's Weekly*, 1874. Built in 1802, the building was purchased by the African American members of First Baptist Church in 1841. It was demolished and replaced in 1876. *Author's collection.*

Long a Richmond landmark, the former First African Baptist Church building at College and Broad Streets is now owned by Virginia Commonwealth University. It was built in 1876 and the congregation met there until the 1950s, when it was moved to the north side of Richmond.

African American church in Richmond. The importance of the structure itself cannot be overestimated. The church building was the grandest structure many black Richmonders knew; it was the place where they could all lay aside their labors and congregate for song, fellowship and a demonstration of faith.

Those who worshipped there included many who rose to prominence, including Maggie Walker, John Jasper, Gilbert Hunt, Henry "Box" Brown and others. Moreover, the church was the center of black cultural and legal life, in that civil matters were often adjudicated there by church leaders.

The establishment of First African Baptist Church as a racially separate entity was typical of similar trends in the antebellum South during that decade. The population of African Americans in cities had increased to the point (as seen with First African Baptist) that they had outgrown their old facilities in the face of religious evangelism that swept the country in the 1840s. It is also noteworthy that African Americans often included the word "African" in the name of the rapidly increasing church denominations and organizations, signaling a close association of religion and race.[6]

An examination of the older African American Richmond churches confirms a close connection with the building arts and the focus of social and religious life for blacks in the city—their church. Often in church histories African American architects and builders play a major role in the stories of the congregations as they contribute to the very fabric of the church itself. These buildings embodied the pride of the African American neighborhoods they served. Their design and decoration were a celebration by the congregation as they moved away from slavery and subjugation.

Third Street Bethel AME Church is one of the oldest black houses of worship in the city. It is shown here in a nineteenth-century photograph. *Courtesy members of the church.*

In the context of African American neighborhoods in the post–Civil War South, churches were true sanctuaries, where the spiritual and temporal needs of the community were met. Church revivals were great religious and social events, often drawing the whole town. Baptisms brought family and neighbors closer. Indeed, church membership framed almost everyone's daily life. In churches many young people met the men or women whom they later courted and married. Churches were safe spaces for political activities and often housed the earliest meetings of the local National Association for the Advancement of Colored People (NAACP).[7] It is no small wonder that the church building itself would be remembered with fondness and reverence, and that the structure would embody the hopes and aspirations of the African American community it served.

These neighborhood churches often sought parity with white congregations in the quality of their facilities, and in many ways the buildings were indistinguishable from each other. Nevertheless, African American churches were a definite expression of their own philosophy and attitudes. Many congregations have followed the classic path of movement from their original sites and have moved to more modern facilities. Still, there are several historically important old churches and their still-thriving congregations remain beacons of pride and major expressions of African American architecture in Richmond. Chief among them is Sixth Mt. Zion Baptist Church.

Established in the most humble of buildings, Sixth Mt. Zion was fueled by one of the most charismatic personalities of African American church history in Richmond. Founded in 1867 by John Jasper and Peter Randolph, this congregation was a direct offshoot of the large First African Baptist Church. A history of Sixth Mt. Zion depicts this first building as being a simple structure, symbolic of the hard times that African Americans in Richmond were subjected to during Reconstruction.[8] Jasper's personality was such that this tiny chapel could not contain his fervent preaching style, made famous by his "De Sun do Move" sermon, which was widely printed and distributed. His oratorical skills created a demand for large space, and after using a carpenter shop and a rented room on Cary Street, the congregation looked for a permanent building.[9]

A former Presbyterian church on the corner of Duval and St. John's Streets was acquired in 1869 from a white congregation that moved from what was rapidly becoming the African American neighborhood of Jackson Ward.[10] Under Jasper's leadership the congregation outgrew the building. A handsome new church, dedicated in 1890, was constructed on the site. The contractor was John Boyd, a prominent African American builder credited with the Maggie Walker house at 110½ East Leigh Street. Boyd's work at Sixth Mt. Zion represents nineteenth-century African American architecture in Richmond.[11] A correspondent from the *Richmond Planet* was in attendance to describe the new church building at its dedication ceremony in 1890:

> *The galleries present a handsome appearance…The windows contain stained glass… In the windows at the rear of the pulpit are pictures of Christ and the Virgin Mary, almost life size…In the cupola is a deep toned bell…The iron supports of the gallery are handsomely bronzed…The total cost of the edifice is $22,000…The seating capacity is estimated at 1,400.*[12]

A week later, a sermon was preached in the new sanctuary by the Reverend Jacob Turner using the highly appropriate text from Second Chronicles: "Now mine eyes shall be opened and mine ears attend unto the prayer that is made in this place."[13] The congregation's ability to lavish so much attention and money on the design and decoration of Sixth Mt. Zion is a testimony to both Jasper's leadership and the growing African American presence in Jackson Ward.

Consistent with the connection between the emotional value of the fabric of the church building itself and the faith that filled it, the *Richmond Planet* article went on to note that the original steps to the building were constructed of wood. John Jasper felt it would be more appropriate that the steps be constructed of stone. He personally donated the stone steps at a cost of more than $200.[14]

Jasper himself lived at 1118 North St. James Street, in a two-story frame house that offered as humble an appearance as the character of the man himself when it was pictured in *Souvenir Views of Negro Enterprises and Residences* in 1907. Jasper's house was lost in the general destruction of his neighborhood in the 1950s by the construction of the same highway that almost claimed his church.

Jasper's history has become part of Sixth Mt. Zion's church building, just as his ministry became a cornerstone of the congregation. In 1926 a John Jasper Memorial Room and Museum was established on the ground floor of the church. Dedicated to the memory of the charismatic preacher, the room preserves the story of his ministry and other artifacts from the long history of the church. It is fitting that the church building in effect rests on this shrine to Jasper and those ministers who followed him.[15]

By 1925, long after the death of the Sixth Mt. Zion's minister in 1901, the church had continued to grow and prosper. The renovations were designed by Charles T. Russell and the Richmond builder I. Lincoln Bailey. Bailey was a member of the congregation; Russell was a deacon of nearby Ebenezer Baptist Church. An undated advertisement noting his office and residence at 8 Baker Street in Jackson Ward also lists Bailey as being both designer and builder of four African American churches in Virginia and South Carolina.[16]

The renovated Sixth Mt. Zion Church at 100 Duval Street is a Gothic revival structure that conveys the dignity of this well-established congregation. Russell and Bailey enlarged the sanctuary and added two towers, redesigned the entrance and also added an educational wing. The additions to the structure can clearly be seen from the east and west sides, giving an idea of the scale of the original building compared to Russell's changes. The historic church continues to serve its Jackson Ward community, with some members traveling many miles back to the city to worship at Sixth Mt. Zion Baptist Church.

A graphic testimony to the importance of this church and its rich history can be seen in the curve that Interstate 95 takes around the site. When it was designed in 1957, the road took a bend to avoid the demolition of this landmark. Sixth Mt. Zion stands above the highway on a concrete cliff, on a strong foundation laid by Jasper. The contributions of generations of African American parishioners as members, builders and supporters throughout the years only strengthen its walls. In 2004 the City of Richmond designated the

Founded in 1867 in a former Confederate horse stable on Brown's Island, Sixth Mt. Zion moved to Jackson Ward two years later where it flourished under the charismatic leadership of the Reverend John Jasper. African American contractor John Boyd built a new church, which was dedicated in 1890. In 1925, architect Charles T. Russell and builder Lincoln Bailey renovated the building in the Gothic revival style.

church a "City Old and Historic District," a zoning overlay that offers the church its highest protection against demolition or inappropriate alteration.

Not far from Sixth Mt. Zion Baptist Church is a small urban park in the 700 block of North First Street, between Duval and Jackson Streets. Nothing remarkable to the casual observer, it is an open lot with a small monument inside a fence enclosure. Only the presence of a bell suspended in a metal framework indicates the historic nature of the site. This is where the St. Joseph's Catholic Church and Van de Vyver School once stood and the site of the first Catholic congregation formed for African Americans in the American South. A brick Gothic church was constructed on the site in the mid-1880s and a complex of buildings followed that included a parish house, a Franciscan convent and the Van de Vyver Institute, which was a church school.[17]

Later known as the Van de Vyver College, the school was named for the bishop of Richmond from 1888 to 1911.[18] This school graduated thirty-five hundred black students in fifty years, providing critical skills and education. A notice of the opening of the college in 1911 described the building as "massive and imposing structures of reinforced concrete and brick, lighted by electricity, heated by steam and equipped with every modern convenience."[19] Charles M. Robinson, who designed many Richmond schools of the period, was the architect for the building. Notable for its arched main entryway, the Van de Vyver College looked like many of the other Robinson schools that still stand in Richmond.[20]

The college was a facility offering a complete education for young African Americans, the curriculum including such things as history, civic government, music, penmanship, business and domestic care services. An innovative portion of the education offered to young men was an automotive school, "enabling any young colored man to become not mere drivers only, but thorough mechanics."[21] The entire course of study was in the context of spiritual instruction as well, and to "form men and women, who, by their virtue and noble aspirations, as well as by their thrifty and industrious habits, will exert a widespread influence on their families and people."[22] The Van de Vyver College and St. Joseph's Church existed until 1969, when Bishop John J. Russell announced its closure. In February 1973 the school building was damaged by fire and it and the church were demolished.[23] Of the complex of buildings, which took up an entire city block, only the former Franciscan nuns' convent on the corner of First and Duvall Streets still stands.

The loss of this facility after its fifty-year history of service to African Americans in Richmond was an enormous blow for the black community on both a practical and sentimental level. Many graduates of the Van de Vyver College still fondly remembered where they received a practical and spiritual education on First Street in Jackson Ward. In 1997, the Catholic diocese and school alumni established St. Joseph's Memorial Park where the college and church once stood. The original bell of St. Joseph's Church was incorporated into the memorial, preserving the memory of this once important African American institution and house of worship.

Also standing on the northern edge of the downtown portion of Jackson Ward is another church with a long history, one whose walls have sheltered many of the leaders of the African American community for decades.

Ebenezer Baptist Church, at 214 West Leigh Street, was founded in 1858 as a daughter congregation of First African Baptist Church, its mission being to serve the growing numbers of free blacks who were moving into Jackson Ward on the eve of the Civil War.[24] That year a frame church on the site of the present structure was dedicated. This church was found to be inadequate for the growing congregation and a brick Gothic structure replaced it in 1873.[25]

Today the church organ in the sanctuary has become an integral part of its architecture as much as it is a part of the service and worship. The curtains of organ pipes form the visual backdrop to the baptismal font and the pulpit. Ebenezer Baptist Church was an innovator in this field and can claim to be the home of the first organ in an African American church in Richmond, installed in 1875. That this congregation could fund this kind of expense for its church so soon after its establishment and in the depths of a national depression in the mid-1870s is testimony to its members' perseverance and faith.[26]

As building inspector for Richmond, Henry Beck condemned many of the city's tall church steeples during his tenure from 1907 to 1912, and Ebenezer Baptist Church was no exception.[27] The truncated steeple tower stood until 1915, when Russell redesigned the front façade of the structure at a cost of $20,000.[28] This changed the decoration of the church from Victorian Gothic to the neoclassical style favored by Russell, and the truncated steeple tower was changed to a cupola with four small spires. In the process of altering the entrance, Russell also created a transitional stair from the sanctuary level to the sidewalk inside the new classical portico.

Just as Ebenezer was the daughter of First African Baptist, the Jackson Ward church has, in turn, spawned many congregations in Richmond and as far away as Hanover County.[29] The church is a landmark on busy Leigh Street and the congregation continues to play an important role in the changing life of Jackson Ward.

St. Joseph's Memorial Park in the 700 block of North First Street. This bell marks the site of the church and the Van De Vyver College, which were both demolished in 1973 after a fifty-year history as the first congregation for black Catholics in the American South. *Photo by author.*

Ebenezer Baptist Church has long been a mainstay in the Jackson Ward area of the city. Charles T. Russell redesigned the front façade to reflect a more classical style.

Manchester, formerly Richmond's sister city on the south side of the James River, combined with Richmond in 1910. The First African Baptist Church, Manchester, traces its roots to the establishment of a prayer group in a private home on Decatur Street in 1823. From this humble beginning, the Manchester church moved to steadily larger accommodations as its congregation and assets grew to afford or construct larger and grander churches. First African Baptist Church of Manchester's second home was termed a "slab building," which may describe a structure with horizontal plank siding on Seventh Street.[30] Opposite the frame building on Seventh Street was a brick church formerly used by a white Methodist congregation. This unnamed group probably felt the industrialization of the lower Manchester area displacing their members and moved, leaving First African Baptist to acquire the building in the early 1850s.[31]

No image exists of the former Methodist church that was acquired for the rapidly growing congregation. Nor does photographic evidence exist for the next building purchased for First African Baptist, "a brick meeting house, 40 x 60," which was constructed nearby. This building appears in an 1865 photograph of lower Manchester and is a substantial temple-form structure rising above a cluster of small, frame houses. It was obviously a major building in this part of Manchester and no doubt visible for some distance from the heights of Richmond across the river.[32]

A photograph of the Reverend Anthony Binga Jr. in the Reverend William Ransome's history of First African Baptist shows a substantial raised central pulpit above an offering table flanked by chairs for deacons and visiting speakers. Two oil lamps on stands illuminate the pulpit from either side, while a heavily draped lectern holds the Bible.[33] The visual focus of the congregation was thus centered on the pulpit, Bible and speaker. The decorative pulpit in front of Binga in the photograph probably reflects the growing sophistication and wealth of the congregation. A church history proudly notes that this was the first building actually constructed by church members.[34]

It is a testimony to the growth of African American Baptists of Manchester and their church that by the 1880s another building program was underway. Lower Manchester was a thriving community of blacks on the edge of the industrial area where no doubt many members of First African Baptist worked. The mills and railroad yards of Manchester were the economic engine that allowed the church to construct another larger brick building, which was dedicated in 1881. An illustration of this structure shows it to be of simple design with double entrances on Perry Street, with a basement level. A small, frame belfry is above the front of the church.[35] Church tradition holds that Binga himself provided the initial architectural design, drawing it on a chalkboard.[36]

The 1881 church was quickly superseded by the present building at Fifteenth and Decatur Streets. Again, Binga is credited with the architectural design, reflecting his central position as spiritual leader of the church and author of the very structure that shelters the congregation. This unique combination of roles for the pastor of First Baptist underscores the independence and pride of this congregation. Binga apparently returned to his chalkboard to design the present building, and the plans were translated into working drawings by a parishioner who had architectural training.[37]

A reporter for the *Richmond Planet* traveled to Manchester to examine the new church constructed by First Baptist and commented that:

> *The First Baptist Church building of Manchester, Reverend A. Binga, Jr., D.D. pastor, is quite unlike the former edifice on Perry Street. The large brick structure with its stately tower made us feel that we had made a mistake and gone to the wrong place to find where these people worshipped. For outside structural beauty, there is no church in the state to excel it...Reverend Binga and his people have undertaken a grand work, and we wish them unlimited success.*[38]

The new building, whose cornerstone was laid in 1892, combines classical and Italianate elements. Today the impressive tower mentioned in the *Richmond Planet* article has a flat top where it originally was topped by a steeple. A severe windstorm on September 29, 1896, damaged many buildings in Richmond. The storm tore the steeples off churches all over the city and blew roofs off entire blocks of houses.[39] Because a city ordinance forbade its replacement, the steeple was not rebuilt.[40]

Binga held that just as his church was the foundation of the spiritual community, economic success was a vital goal for Manchester's African Americans. The history of the church and its various facilities in what is now south Richmond reflects the presence of carpenters and craftsmen within the congregation. "Dr. Binga taught that people should acquire property, especially for a home for their families," wrote Ransome, who succeeded

Binga as minister. Many of the older homes of Manchester were probably constructed with Binga's admonitions in mind. He stressed the close connection between church, community and home ownership. The building crafts practiced by African Americans in Manchester became the bedrock of owner-occupied neighborhoods who were served in turn by First Baptist.

A case in point illustrating Binga's philosophy is the First African Baptist Church parsonage. A church history written in the 1930s noted that most of the large homes in the area were already owned with Binga's encouragement by parishioners of First Baptist. "After much discussion and some intense feeling, it was decided to erect the parsonage on the lot which adjoins the church lot."[41] Plans for the house were drawn by architect Charles Russell, who had made a specialty of designing churches and church renovations and was a logical choice for the assignment. It was apparently a priority for the congregation that their new parsonage be built and designed by African Americans as "great effort was made to secure a Negro contractor."[42] Although much effort was made to obtain bids by a black contractor, their bids exceeded the funds available. In a compromise, a white firm, Bass & Brothers, was finally awarded the contract for construction of the building, although the church stipulated that the white firm had "to hire a reasonable amount of Negro labor."[43]

This stipulation underscores again the intense connection between the works of the church, its philosophy of self-sufficiency promoted by Binga in the church community and the pride and confidence felt in the construction of the new parsonage. The 1935 church history proudly notes that much of the construction was done by parishioners, including the plastering and painting. Ed Perry, the chairman of the usher board, dug the foundations of the new building.[44] A list was compiled of over four hundred parishioners, fraternal organizations and clubs who donated money to the construction of the parsonage, and contributions as small as twenty-five cents were carefully and proudly recorded.[45]

The resulting parsonage, which was built at 1507 Decatur Street, was dedicated with much ceremony on January 15, 1922. The house designed by Russell was typical of many of the others in the neighborhood, combining classical and Italianate elements. It reflected not only Russell's abilities as an architect, but also the intense pride felt by the members of First Baptist Church, south Richmond. Their hard-earned pennies financed the parsonage, a noted architect of their own race designed it and much of the fabric of the building was constructed by their own hands. Unfortunately, this house was at some point demolished and the lot used to expand the church facilities. Nevertheless, its history remains a fundamental part of the First Baptist Church story. The parsonage is gone, but the spirit that built the houses and populated the African American neighborhoods around the church remains.

Ransome continued to promote Binga's philosophy regarding home ownership and confirming the ties between the ministry of the south Richmond church and the built environment around it. He stressed the concept of neighborhood and church, and fought against the arrival of the subsidized public housing such as that built in the area of the Manchester Courthouse at Decatur Street. "Scrub floors and wash dishes, if you must," Ransome exhorted the members of First Baptist, "but work and own your own home."[46]

A cooperative history project initiated in 1990 between First Baptist Church, south Richmond, and Virginia Commonwealth University yielded a two-volume history of the church and its congregations over the years. Under the direction of Dr. LaVerne Byrd Smith, church historian, material was collected on African American neighborhoods in south Richmond. The areas where Binga and Ransome so strongly urged their parishioners to live and buy their own homes were concentrated in the neighborhoods of Blackwell and the lesser-known areas of Swansboro and Newtown South.[47] An examination of the tiny but proud neighborhood of Newtown South and its housing stock will demonstrate the homes typical of those the ministers of First Baptist Church so carefully nurtured and promoted.

Newtown South has been defined by a resident as

> *a unique little village in Manchester. It is two blocks wide and six streets deep, nestled between the Atlantic Coast Line railroad property and Vaden's Property bordering east and west respectively and by Hull and Everett streets running north and south.*[48]

The streets that compose Newtown are short sections of city streets, interrupted by industrial sites on every side. The houses along East Plinkton Street and the tiny side streets that compose the neighborhood are small, comfortable, working-class bungalows from the early part of the 1900s, most with low front porches. The neighborhood is an island of charm and tree-shaded streets just off the faded outer business district that was once downtown Manchester. A small city park and one of the cross streets in Newtown were renamed for Marion Mashore, honoring the legacy of a longtime community activist.

If Newtown South was a village unto itself, then the village church was Second Baptist Church, south Richmond, located at 105 East Plinkton Street in the middle of the community. The congregation was established in 1880.[49] The current small, Gothic revival brick church was erected in 1905. Its slender and graceful belfry rises above the low houses of Newtown.

While Newtown South languished in neglect for many years, a number of residents remember it as an energetic and thriving community:

> *There were five grocery stores, several beauticians, and barbers for both white and black men, seamstresses, plumbers, wallpaper hangers, a transfer hauling company, and oil men. There also were teachers, ministers, a railway clerk, and in later years, a funeral home was added.*[50]

Emblematic of the spirit of Newtown South is the small bungalow at 2406 Everett Street. It is a nicely kept brick home with a welcoming front porch and was once no doubt one in a series of homes along that eastern side of Everett. Unfortunately, encroachment of the factory behind it has claimed its neighbors. Tall, barbed wire fences loom over the house at

This is the latest of several sanctuaries constructed by the growing congregation of First Baptist, south Richmond, in what was known as the city of Manchester.

2406 Everett Street on three sides of the property line. Nevertheless, like Newtown South itself, this house survives.

In an effort to retain the types of residents who have called Newtown South home, affordable, new, architecturally sensitive infill has replaced the houses that have been lost over the years, under the guidance of the Newtown Civic Improvement League. "The families in the village were very close and a very caring group of people," reminisced a Newtown South old-timer.[51] Judging by the care with which many of these small, neat homes are tended, the spirit of Newtown will continue into the future, fueled by a sense of history and community pride. Moreover, it reflects the central role of churches in the development of African American neighborhoods.

11

Richmond's
African American Cemeteries

"A Hard Road to Glory"
—Inscription on the tombstone of Arthur Ashe

The cemetery is an expression of sentiment, status and religious faith, as much as the homes, businesses and churches of Richmond. A discussion of the architecture created for or by blacks in Richmond would be incomplete without an examination of the city's cemeteries. All funerary architecture, be it a marker with an inscription drawn by hand in wet cement or a high-style mausoleum, is intended to be permanent. Unfortunately, in many cases in the African American community the monuments to the dead have been lost over the years.

Veronica A. Davis, author of one of the few works on black cemeteries in Richmond, noted that the damage of years of neglect has been done and there is now but one recourse open to those who would preserve this part of black history. Writing about her reaction when she first viewed the cemeteries, Davis said:

> I could not believe my eyes when I looked upon so many overgrown graves around Richmond. Upon visiting the cemeteries at Evergreen, I grew angry at the native black Richmonders, but myself as well. There are not one or two people responsible for the death of black cemeteries, but an entire race. Sure, we could spend years finger-pointing and looking the other way, or we could spend just as much time ourselves lifting a rake, water hose, repairing our cemeteries and keeping them memorable.[1]

The earliest known African American cemetery in Richmond is the Burial Ground for Negroes in Shockoe Valley in the 1500 block of East Broad Street. Countless African Americans were buried at this location, along with those who were executed at the public gallows, which stood on the same site. Shockoe Creek once ran through the deep ravine where the burial ground is located. The burial ground appears on Richard Young's map of Richmond (1790–1809). Here Gabriel, the leader of an unsuccessful slave rebellion, was hanged with his conspirators on October 10, 1800. In 2004, this site received recognition in a state historical marker on the Broad Street sidewalk.[2]

A Richard Young Map of Richmond, 1809. Courtesy Library of Virginia.

Detail of the Richard Young map showing the Burial Ground for Negroes, located on today's Broad Street in Shockoe Valley. Courtesy Library of Virginia.

The funerary markers of slavery-era blacks were, because of constraints imposed on an enslaved people, both crude and impermanent. Frederick Law Olmsted, a famous landscape architect and social commentator of the nineteenth century, wrote of his travels through the American South and, in the course of a visit to Richmond, described the funeral of a slave child at a "desolate place" beyond the neat and tidy white burying ground. At the funeral, Olmsted found himself "deeply influenced...by the unaffected feeling, in connection with the simplicity, natural, rude truthfulness, and absence of all attempt at formal decorum in the crowd."[3] He went on to describe how a grave was marked, and this may be typical of the extent to which the resting places of slaves were commemorated. He wrote:

> *A man had, in the mean time, gone into a ravine near by, and now returned with two small branches, hung with withered leaves, that he had broken off a beech tree; these were placed upright, one at the head, the other at the foot of the grave.*[4]

Clearly, with scant markings such as this example and with the few and perishable materials available to them, many enslaved Richmonders were unable to mark the graves of their dead in a way that we can see and study today. African American cemeteries were often ignored when they stood in the course of what was termed "progress." At the end of the Civil War, detonation by Federal authorities of a city powder magazine located in the area began the destruction of the nearby black cemetery that Olmsted visited.[5] The bridge that carries Fifth Street covered the burying ground that Olmsted saw. The demolition of the bridge and its reconstruction in the 1990s only served to further erase all traces of an unknown number of African American graves that once filled the hillside above Bacon's Quarter Branch, a ravine on the northern perimeter of the city.

Insensitivity toward the preservation of well-established African American cemeteries continued in the years after the Civil War. In her book, Davis enumerates many of these neglected cemeteries in Richmond, such as the Young Sons of Ham graveyard behind Bandy Field in Richmond's West End.[6] There are clearly other graves beside the two solitary gravestones left in the Sons of Ham cemetery marking the last resting place of Queen V. Johnston (1875–1900) and Moses Bradford, a Spanish-American War veteran who died in 1936. The Johnston stone depicts the gates of heaven opening (a common funerary image), whereas the Bradford stone is a distinctive, government-issue marker with the shield device particular to graves of veterans of that war.[7]

Many of the members of Gravel Hill Baptist Church at 2600 Gravel Hill Road in south Richmond were workers in the stone quarries at the nearby train stop known as Granite, and the abandoned quarries are still visible near the modern Willow Oaks Country Club off Forest Hill Avenue. The unmarked graves in a small African American cemetery at 6911 Old Westham Road may hold some of the quarry workers who helped create many of the enduring granite buildings and street features in Richmond.

Few graves in the cemetery retain markers, and they must be hunted among the vines and fallen trees that litter the site. The graves of members of the Carrington family are marked with distinctive headstones made of cement, with crude inscriptions lettered in the concrete of the marker after it was poured into a mold. In the setting of the overgrown and trash-strewn cemetery, the epitaph on the two Carrington markers, "Gone But Not Forgotten," is ironic. Despite the crude construction and lettering on the markers, the use of the omega symbol as a decorative device below the epitaph hints at a level of sophistication and education on the part of the craftsman of the two markers. Hemmed in on three sides by a gas station, a suburban home and a fast food restaurant, this cemetery is listed on City of Richmond tax rolls as "abandoned." However, despite its derelict appearance, the recent placement of artificial flowers on a grave there signals that there are those who are very much aware of the cemetery's existence.[8]

While the cemetery on Old Westham Road still has stones marking the graves, the tiny African American cemetery at 9550 Evansway Lane, off Stony Point Road in south Richmond, has nothing left to tell the story of the people buried there. Once located in a rural setting along a farm road, the small plot is now wedged between two tri-level homes. Only the creeping ivy characteristic of neglected cemeteries and a few sunken gravesites indicate the reason this small patch of woods was preserved from development. Devoid of decoration or marker, the tiny plot is recognized as a city cemetery only by tax records.

The abandonment of historic African American cemeteries is common in all parts of Richmond. The removal of the headstones in the cemetery behind Westwood Baptist Church was an enormous historic loss wherein much information about the earliest residents of the neighborhood was lost. Today, only a single marker commemorates the unknown number of early burials in Westwood.

The Westwood community currently uses a cemetery located on a large plot several miles west of the neighborhood behind the Toys "R" Us store at 8700 Quioccasin Road. This once rural area is now hemmed in by suburban sprawl. Among the many African American graves found there are those of the family of Virginia State Senator Benjamin J. Lambert III. The earliest graves in the "new" Westwood cemetery, like that of Bettie Fountain, date to the era of World War I. Despite the fact that this is a comparatively modern cemetery, many graves are marked only with flat stones at head and foot, a funeral practice harking back to the earliest days of anonymous slave burials.

Two black cemeteries in particular are examples of how free African Americans constructed memorials to their dead and defined the grounds of these areas. In the Barton Heights neighborhood, a series of adjoining cemeteries was established beginning in the early part of the nineteenth century with a burying ground on what was then called Academy Hill.[9] From this original site six cemeteries were laid out on adjoining plots, the whole of which is generally known today as the Barton Heights Cemetery.[10]

The term "mechanics" once referred to the trades in general, and the name of Union Mechanics Cemetery indicates that this was the resting place for the black, upper-class builders, plasterers and carpenters of the time. The important status of these professionals can be demonstrated by the fact that in 1901 the distinguished Reverend John Jasper of Sixth Mt. Zion Baptist Church, whose funeral attracted thousands to the Barton Heights Cemetery, was buried alongside the many tradesmen.

The grave of Moses Bradford (1869–1936) in the tiny abandoned African American cemetery at Bandy Field on Three Chopt Road. Bradford was a Spanish-American War veteran who was disabled while fighting in Cuba. *Photo by author.*

In the years prior to World War I, the decline of the Union Mechanics Cemetery led to Jasper's remains being relocated to the more fashionable and then better-tended Woodland Cemetery in the East End. Today an obelisk carved by John Henry Brown, one of Richmond's foremost black stonemasons, marks the site of Jasper's burial. Brown's mark can be seen on the left side of the base of the monument, a small reminder of the craftsman who created what must have been one of his most important commissions.[11]

As the Barton Heights Cemetery continued to decline and become overgrown, vandals took a toll on the monuments that were supposed to stand forever in memory of thousands of Richmond's African American residents. "Every councilman," commented the *Richmond News Leader* in 1934,

> along with every other citizen, has been conscious of a certain sense of humiliation whenever he looked at the overgrown, neglected Negro cemeteries at the north end of the First Street bridge. They were an eyesore as well as a reproach to a city that is usually most careful in keeping its burial grounds in order.[12]

Blacks who owned plots in the cemetery added their voices to the demands for action.

In the same year the city took steps to condemn "the old burying ground, the resting place of many faithful Negro servants of a former day," clean up the site and continue to use it as a municipal cemetery.[13] Despite the acquisition by the city, the area continued to be overgrown and its markers and monuments disappeared or were vandalized. Hundreds of gravestones were lost. Lost with them were the names and dates of the deceased, as well as the craftsmanship, design and detailing of markers intended to honor the dead.

Fortunately, the Barton Heights Cemetery has been stabilized, despite the loss of much of its fabric. An initiative in 1992, spearheaded by Denise Lester, resulted in clearance of much of the trees and underbrush from the grounds, and many of the surviving markers were revealed for the first time in years. At the time, Lester, a descendant of one of the cemetery's organizers, was conducting genealogical research. Continuing stewardship by Lester's Burial Ground Society of Virginia has resulted in the fencing of the cemetery and its being placed on the Virginia Register of Historic Landmarks.[14] An annual Whit Monday ceremony brings people to the Barton Heights Cemetery, affirming it as the only real success story in the history of the reclamation of African American cemeteries in Richmond.[15]

Gilbert Hunt is buried at Cedarwood Cemetery in what is now called Barton Heights. Hunt became a local hero for his rescue of victims of an 1811 theater fire, now memorialized by Monumental Church on Broad Street. *Courtesy Valentine Richmond History Center.*

Another black cemetery of enormous importance and one whose stock of monuments and memorials has recently reemerged from overgrowth is Woodland Cemetery in the far East End. Founded by *Richmond Planet* editor John Mitchell Jr. in 1918, the cemetery was laid out on forty acres on Magnolia Road. Mitchell himself is credited with the design of the roads and arrangement of the burial plots.[16] This cemetery, too, was virtually lost in a jungle of trees and served as a dumping ground for construction debris and appliances. It is, nevertheless, the burial place of some of Richmond's leading African Americans. Reverend John Jasper's granite obelisk still guards his remains, although its once-commanding knoll is now shared by the maintenance building for the cemetery.

Today the woods have been forced back from the grounds of Woodland and it is again possible to imagine the cemetery in its original splendor with roads and curbings intact and the decorated graves of many notable Richmond African Americans dotting the landscape below Jasper's tomb. This is the cemetery that Mitchell proudly showed off to black leader Marcus Garvey in 1922 when he took Garvey on a tour of Richmond in his Stanley Steamer automobile. Along the way he pointed out the accomplishments of African Americans in the city to his distinguished visitor.[17]

Much of the reclamation of Woodland Cemetery is credited to the burial of Arthur Ashe, one of the most prominent tennis players of all time. Growing up in segregated Richmond, he was forbidden to play on the city's courts, which at the time were reserved for whites only. After his untimely death in 1993, Ashe's body was returned from New York to Richmond for burial at Woodland Cemetery. Ashe must have been cognizant of the decline of the cemetery where his family members were interred, but he still insisted on being buried there. His black granite monument with the epitaph "A Hard Road to Glory" stands beside the smaller stone marking the grave of his mother, Mattie. Nearby is also the grave of Ashe's beloved grandmother, Jimmie Cunningham.

Another endangered cemetery in Richmond is the East End Cemetery, established in 1897. The carefully laid out concrete walks of the cemetery now disappear into the woods, with only the corner markers protruding from the carpet of leaves indicating where many plots are located. The cemetery covers a six-acre area and only a tiny portion of that is visible from the road. Entry into the interior is impossible except where family members have cleared a passage through the underbrush to a specific cemetery section. East End Cemetery, once termed "the place to be buried," retains only a suggestion of order, design and fashion discernable through the underbrush.[18]

Evergreen Cemetery adjoins the East End Cemetery on Stony Run Road and was created in 1891. It was laid out by the Evergreen Cemetery Association on a high ridge overlooking the valley formed by Stony Run and Gillies Creek; it was planned to be the African American equivalent of Richmond's high-style Hollywood Cemetery for whites. From below, dense woods obscure the effect of the massed monuments on its hillside, and the historic gravestones extend deep into the woods, where the dead are forgotten amid overgrown paths, upturned monuments and anonymous graves. The entrance to Evergreen Cemetery does not suggest its past glories as the black Hollywood either. Evergreen, which must have been a showplace of funerary architecture and design at the time of its inception,

International tennis star Arthur Ashe chose to be buried in Woodland Cemetery, founded in 1918 by John Mitchell Jr. *Photo by author.*

has been obscured over time by vandals and nature. The modern section of the cemetery is an open field where the temporary markers of those who cannot afford gravestones are routinely destroyed by lawn mowers. The farthest end of the open area at Evergreen is a dumping ground for excavated dirt and was even the resting place for the remains of a bullet-riddled city vehicle.

On a knoll in Evergreen Cemetery overlooking Fulton Bottom is the memorial to the most famous of the notable African Americans buried there. A large granite cross marks the grave of entrepreneur Maggie L. Walker. There was an intense outpouring of grief and respect for Walker at the time of her death in 1934. Thousands of mourners marched on a funeral route from First African Baptist Church to Evergreen Cemetery. The large granite cross erected on the Walker family plot must have been visible on the hillside for some distance above Fulton before the brush and undergrowth took over the view.[19]

In 1984 there was discussion about moving Walker's grave because visitors to Richmond interested in the nation's first black female bank president found her grave inaccessible. One of Walker's granddaughters said, "I used to be against the idea, but now that Evergreen is like a wilderness, I think it might be a good idea."[20] Ultimately, Walker was not moved; she remains among her family members whose gravestones cluster around the large cross.

This large cross in Evergreen Cemetery marks the Walker family plot, the burial place of the first female black bank president, Maggie Lena Walker. Walker died in 1934.

Near the Walker plot is a handsome tombstone, on which is a granite angel embracing a cross. This marks the plot where John Mitchell Jr. and his mother Rebecca are buried. It is appropriate that Mitchell is buried so near Walker, his contemporary, as these two were the most influential black Richmonders of their time. Mitchell's biographer, Ann Field Alexander, noted, "Mitchell was an avid reader of history, and he was keenly aware of the importance of monuments and what historians today call 'memory.'" The monument in all of Richmond dearest to the *Richmond Planet*'s editor was no doubt the grave of Rebecca Mitchell, his mother, who died in 1913. On the base of the marble angel that marks her tomb is engraved her son's extraordinary tribute: "She Hated Deceit and Despised Hypocrisy. Her Christian Training and Upright Conduct Made Me All That I Am—All That I Hoped to Be."

This moving testimonial from a devoted son is now hardly visible under the carpet of weeds and scrub. Mitchell's own grave is located in the same plot as his mother's, but the passage of time since his death has completely obscured the site, and the last resting place of this distinguished Richmonder is impossible to find. All around, the graves of thousands of Richmond's citizens of color stretch off into deep woods, forgotten, obscured and lost to neglect. Evergreen Cemetery, planned with such style and promise, is today a haunting and oppressive place.

Today there are hundreds of overturned grave markers in Evergreen Cemetery. Among them, one is of particular interest in that it is the grave of a man who was instrumental in constructing much of black Richmond's architecture in the early years of the last century. In the hilltop section of the derelict cemetery, near the plots where Walker and Mitchell are buried, is a vine-covered area. Lying neglected where it fell face up in the brush and weeds is a granite pylon with the following inscription below a Masonic symbol:

My Husband
Daniel J. Farrar, Sr.
Master Architect, Contractor & Builder
Oct. 17, 1862
March 10, 1923
Tho lost to sight,
To memory dear.

It is ironic that Farrar's monument has all but disappeared from view. As secretary of the Evergreen Cemetery Association, Farrar would have been convinced of the permanence of the institution. His purchase of a hilltop site, certainly among the most expensive, placed him near the plots of his most famous contemporaries, Walker and Mitchell. His granite monolith, adorned with the compass and square of the Masons, symbolized a durability and status that the passage of time would not erode.

The message that Evergreen first broadcast, that of parity and permanence, has become defused and blunted. The neglected cemetery distresses and confuses its few visitors, and the architecture of what was intended to be a memorial park can affect those who enter it. Dr. Jack Spiro, a professor at Virginia Commonwealth University who lectures on issues of death and mourning, commented that poor cemetery conditions

can have a devastating impact on a grieving person. That's why perpetual care is so important…weeds and broken tombstones represent just what a cemetery is not supposed to represent. The weeds themselves can become symbols of death and decay.[21]

The Braxton mausoleum is one of the few to be found in an African American cemetery. It was probably considered very stylish when constructed in the 1930s, built in the usual temple form common to American mausoleums, but with geometric decoration suggestive of the art deco style. The crisply defined recessed panels in the concrete wall of the monument are decorated with red tile diamonds. Repeatedly opened and ransacked over the years, the concrete block wall that replaced the doorway shows recent signs of attack by vandals, defying the inherent messages of permanence and eternity these small houses of the dead are designed to convey.[22]

A distinctive trait of African American graves in Evergreen, as in most of the black cemeteries around Richmond, is the inscription describing membership in fraternal organizations. This emphasizes the importance of these associations and the status

The graves of Rebecca Mitchell and her son, editor John Mitchell Jr., are in Evergreen Cemetery.

The grave of W.W. Browne, president of the True Reformers Bank, is located in Woodland Cemetery.

conferred by membership. The most overt example of this is the grave of Rosa E. Watson, who died in June 1934. Her gravestone touchingly notes "Friend of Maggie L. Walker" on the front, and above that, advises the visitor to "Read Back of Stone." The entire back side of the grave marker is taken up with the names of organizations to which Watson belonged, such as the "American Beauty Circle No. 30" and the "Matrons Board of Richmond Va." The inscriptions record a busy life filled with activities and interest in her community, perhaps confirmed by the inscription above Watson's name: "At Rest."

It was sometimes the custom for white employers to provide gravestones for their workers, enabling them to be credited with the memorial and to dictate the content of the inscription. The substantial gravestone of Nannie Newton, who died in 1925, is labeled, "Erected by the Elam family in remembrance of her long faithful service." The name of George Newton, who died in 1913, is added below this inscription as though an afterthought. Some may question the desirability of this commemoration of years of service to the Elam family, which could easily have extended back into the slavery era.

Other headstones note the donor of the monument as being a church body, such as a deacon board. The headstone for George W. Price, who died in 1924, is marked, "By Porters of Broad St. Station," perhaps the last favor for a dead colleague. This type of gravestone is an interesting example of the funerary architecture of cemeteries such as Evergreen.

Less informative, but no less interesting, are the decorative schemes of some of the borders of plots whose size is defined by concrete curbings. Small tiles of the type commonly used in house construction that identify the family or original owner of the plot decorate a number of these curbings in Evergreen Cemetery. The plot labeled H.H. Allen is typical of the more humble decoration, with the name defined in small black and white tiles decorating the low post beside the threshold into the Allen plot. Another plot nearby, labeled in the same small tiles and apparently by the same hand, identifies the burial ground of Austin Stevens.

The funerary architecture seen on other graves conveys different types of information about the dead and displays a spectrum of styles and influences. Veronica Davis, in her book, credits the seashells that surround the marker of William H. Watson's grave as being indicative of an African influence or that of African American decorative practices from the Deep South.[23] The nearby grave of John J. Bly, in contrast, is awash with classical influences and iconography. An urn with flames emerging from the top is draped with a shroud and a wreath of flowers. These, in turn, stand on a base covered with a fringed cloth and decorated with garlands—all executed in marble. The Bly marker stands slightly downhill from the circle where the Walker cross is surrounded by deep woods. The execution of all these decorative elements, although they are somewhat weathered, is beautifully done and, when erected in 1911, must have been stunning on the hillside above the valley.

From the ruined temporary markers left by funeral homes to the elaborate monuments of the African American elite of yesterday, the gravestones of Evergreen Cemetery are impressive. Whole sections of the cemetery are covered with the creeping vine kudzu, and it is evident that visitors frequently come to Evergreen to beat back the rapidly moving vines from their family plots that cover the markers of their dead like a green tide. In other sections, empty graves seem to signal where caskets have been removed to some better-tended site. It is disconcerting and defies commonly held beliefs about the care of the dead, their monuments and the grounds where they lie.

The architecture of the dead at Evergreen and Richmond's other black cemeteries is an important record. Unfortunately, many of these sites are disappearing. Preservationists say the most imperiled burial grounds are those historically used by African Americans. They contend that the eighteenth- and nineteenth-century graveyards were often inadequately marked, and many of their occupants were too poor to afford lasting monuments. In many places, the vast twentieth-century immigration of blacks to Northern cities depopulated many rural Southern towns, leaving black cemeteries hopelessly neglected.[24]

From the anonymous unmarked grave to the polished granite monument of an international sports star, each of these Richmond sites has a history and represents a window into African American culture. As such, they should be treasured and preserved, not just to honor the past but also to inform the future.

Notes

1. The Beginning

1. Harry M. Ward, *Richmond, An Illustrated History* (Northridge, CA: Windsor Publications, 1985), 14.
2. Marie Tyler-McGraw, *At the Falls: Richmond, Virginia and Its People* (Chapel Hill: Published for the Valentine, the Museum of the Life and History of Richmond, by the University of North Carolina Press, 1994), 19–20.
3. Ibid., 33.
4. John Rolfe noted in a letter to Sir Edward Sandys that the governor of the colony "bought" the Africans. However, the verb "to buy" also meant "to hire." Because indentures usually lasted for seven years, these Africans were most likely engaged for that, or a similar, period of time.
5. Maurice Duke, *Don't Carry Me Back! Narratives by Former Virginia Slaves* (Richmond: Dietz Press, 1995), ix–xi.
6. Peter Kolchin, *American Slavery, 1619–1877* (New York: Hill and Wang, 2003), 10–11.
7. Darrett B. Rutman and Anita H. Rutman, *A Place in Time: Middlesex County, Virginia, 1650–1750* (New York: W.W. Norton and Company, 1984), 69.
8. Carl R. Lounsbury, *An Illustrated Glossary of Early Southern Architecture and Landscape* (New York: Oxford University Press, 1994), 393.
9. Philip D. Morgan, *Slave Counterpoint: Black Culture in the Eighteenth-Century Chesapeake and Lowcountry* (Chapel Hill: University of North Carolina Press, 1998), 105.
10. William Byrd I called his settlement on the James "Shacco's" in his diaries and correspondence. This is the origin of the modern name Shockoe Creek and Shockoe Valley. The settlement was also called simply "Byrd's Warehouse," which underscores the character and purpose of the small community.
11. "Skirmish at Richmond Jan. 5th 1781." Illustrated in Harry M. Ward and Harold E. Greer Jr., *Richmond During the Revolution, 1775–1783* (Charlottesville: University Press of Virginia, 1977), 79.
12. Ibid., 8–9.
13. Johann David Schöpf, *Travels in the Confederation* [1783–1784]. Translated and edited by Alfred J. Morrison. Vol. 2. Reprint, New York, 1968. Quoted in Ward and Greer, *Richmond*, 9–10.
14. John Michael Vlach, "Plantation Landscapes of the Antebellum South." In Edward D.C. Campbell Jr. and Kym S. Rice, eds., *Before Freedom Came: African-American Life in the Antebellum South* (Richmond: The Museum of the Confederacy, 1991), 43.
15. Samuel Mordecai, *Richmond in By-Gone Days* (Richmond: Dietz Press, [reprint of 1946 edition]), 275–76.
16. Charles B. Dew, *Ironmaker to the Confederacy: Joseph R. Anderson and the Tredegar Iron Works* (Richmond: Library of Virginia, 1999), 19–20.

17. Gregg D. Kimball, *American City, Southern Place: A Cultural History of Antebellum Richmond* (Athens: University of Georgia Press, 2000), 171.

18. Ibid., 92; Dew, *Ironmaker*.

19. Midori Takagi, *Rearing Wolves to Our Own Destruction: Slavery in Richmond, Virginia, 1782–1865* (Charlottesville: University Press of Virginia, 1999), 74.

2. The Slave Markets in Shockoe Valley

1. These groups included the City of Richmond, the Richmond Slave Trail Commission, the Virginia Department of Historic Resources and the Alliance to Conserve Old Richmond Neighborhoods (ACORN). The actual excavation, documentation and recovery of artifacts were done by the James River Institute of Archaeology. See "Artifacts Unearthed at Lumpkin's Jail," *Richmond Free Press*, May 11–13, 2006, 1.

2. W.L. Bost, quoted in *Unchained Memories: Readings from the Slave Narratives* (Boston: Bullfinch Press, 2002), 26.

3. On his way from his home in Franklin County to Hampton Institute, Washington later wrote, "By walking, begging rides, and paying for a portion of the journey on the steam-cars, I finally succeeded in reaching the city of Richmond, Virginia, where I was without money or friends. I slept under a sidewalk, and by working on a vessel the next day I earned money to continue my way to the institute, where I arrived with a surplus of fifty cents." Booker T. Washington, "The Awakening of the Negro," *Atlantic Monthly* 78 (September 1896), 322.

4. Kimball, *American City*, 29.

5. Lonnie Bunch, "Slave Auctions," in *Unchained Memories*, 21.

6. Ernest B. Ferguson, *Ashes of Glory: Richmond at War* (New York: Knopf, 1996), 20.

7. Ibid., 21.

8. Ibid.

9. Robert Gudmestad, "The Richmond Slave Market, 1840–1860" (master's thesis, University of Richmond, 1993), 38–40.

10. Ibid., 123.

11. Patricia Lee Brown, "In a Barn, A Piece of Slavery's Hidden Past," *New York Times*, May 6, 2003, A1.

12. Daisy L. Avery, "Slave Market of Hector Davis," June 11, 1937, Works Progress Administration of Virginia Historical Survey, No. 231 Henrico County, Library of Virginia, Richmond City, 3. Avery quotes Davis's advertisement in a Richmond business directory from 1859.

13. Ibid., 2.

14. Ibid.

15. Ibid.

16. Ibid.

17. John S. Wise, *The End of an Era* (Boston: Houghton, Mifflin, 1899), 80–81.

18. Maurice Duke, "Slave Auction Block: Richmond Once Operated One of the Biggest in the World," *Richmond Free Press*, April 8–10, 2004.

19. Charles H. Corey, *A History of the Richmond Theological Seminary, with Reminiscences of Thirty Years' Work Among the Colored People of the South* (Richmond: J.W. Randolph, 1895), 75–76.

20. Ibid., 47.

21. Raymond P. Hylton, "University History," Virginia Union University "About VUU," http://www.vuu.edu/aboutvuu/history.htm.

22. Corey, *Theological Seminary*, 77.

23. Ibid., 47.

24. Matthew R. Laird, PhD, *Preliminary Archaeological Investigation of the Lumpkin's Jail Site* (44HE1053), Richmond, Virginia (Williamsburg, VA: James River Institute for Archaeology, Inc., 2006), ii. Even the most preliminary investigation of the site conducted in 2006 led the architectural team in charge to recommend that Lumpkin's Jail site be nominated to the National Register of Historic Places and led them to state that the potential for future discoveries is enormous. A more extensive survey is to take place in 2007.

25. Mary Wingfield Scott, *Old Richmond Neighborhoods* (Richmond: Valentine Museum, 1984), 86.

26. Douglas R. Edgerton, *Gabriel's Rebellion: The Virginia Slave Conspiracies of 1800 and 1802* (Chapel Hill: University of North Carolina Press, 1993), 111.

27. A state historical marker placed on the Broad Street sidewalk in 2004 confirmed the presence of the Burial Ground for Negroes under the adjacent parking lot.

3. Urban Plantations and the Civil War

1. Nelson Lankford, *Richmond Burning: The Last Days of the Confederate Capital* (New York: Viking, 2002), 16.

2. Kimball, *American City*, 65.

3. Morgan, *Slave Counterpoint*, 355.

4. Ibid., 359.

5. Takagi, *Rearing Wolves*, 39–40.

6. Kimball, *American City*, 65.

7. Lankford, *Richmond Burning*, 15.

8. Richard Guy Wilson, ed., *Buildings of Virginia: Tidewater and Piedmont* (New York: Oxford University Press, 2002), 186.

9. Ibid., 200.

10. Marguerite Crumley and John G. Zehmer, *Church Hill: The St. John's Church Historic District* (Richmond: The Council of Historic Richmond Foundation, 1991), 52.

11. Benjamin Ross et al., *Two Centuries of Christian Witness: The History of Sixth Mount Zion Baptist Church of Richmond, Virginia* (Richmond: Hospitality Committee, Sixth Mt. Zion Baptist Church, n.d.), 11–13.

12. Calder Loth, ed., *The Virginia Landmarks Register*, 4th ed. (Charlottesville: University Press of Virginia, 1999), 437.

13. The term "auctioneer" was used more generally than it is today, and persons in this business often traded in African Americans as another commodity to buy and on which to trade and speculate.

14. Mary Wingfield Scott, *Houses of Old Richmond* (Richmond: Valentine Museum, 1941), 16.

15. Mordecai, *By-Gone Days*, 142.

16. Microfilm copies of this resource are available at the Mutual Assurance Society of Virginia, Declarations and Reevaluations of Assurance 1796–1872, call number 31634, miscellaneous reels 4121–4143, Library of Virginia, Richmond City.

17. Bryan Clark Green et al., *Lost Virginia: Vanished Architecture of the Old Dominion* (Charlottesville, VA: Howell Press, 2001), 49.

18. Scott, *By-Gone Days*, 72.

19. Elizabeth R. Vardon, *Southern Lady, Yankee Spy: The True Story of Elizabeth Van Lew, A Union Agent in the Heart of the Confederacy* (New York: Oxford University Press, 2003), 89.

20. Ibid., 92–93.

21. As a biographer of Walker notes, the actual year of her birth is problematic. See Gertrude Wooruff Marlowe, *A Right Worthy Grand Mission: Maggie Walker and the Quest for Black Economic Empowerment* (Washington, D.C.: Howard University Press, 2003), 1–2.

22. Marie Tyler-McGraw and Gregg D. Kimball, *In Bondage and Freedom: Antebellum Black Life in Richmond, Virginia* (Richmond: Valentine Museum, 1988), 27.

23. Kimball, *American City*, 248.

24. Tyler-McGraw, *At the Falls*, 149.

25. Richard M. Lee, *General Lee's City* (McLean, VA: EPM Publications, 1987), 173.

26. Ibid.

27. Jeffrey R. Kerr-Ritchie, *The Freed People in the Tobacco South: Virginia, 1860–1900* (Chapel Hill: University of North Carolina Press, 1999), 25.

28. Takagi, *Rearing Wolves*, 127.

29. Ibid., 128–30.

30. Peter Rachleff, *Black Labor in Richmond, 1865–1890* (Chicago: University of Illinois Press, 1989), 37.

31. Matthew L. Cushman, "Free Black Barbers in Antebellum Richmond, A Cut Above the Rest" (unpublished seminar paper, Department of Art History, Virginia Commonwealth University, n.d.), 10.

32. Takagi, *Rearing Wolves*, 146.
33. Steven J. Hoffman, *Race, Class and Power in the Building of Richmond, 1870–1920* (Jefferson, NC: McFarland & Co., 2004), 143.

4. Black Entrepreneurs, Designers, Craftsmen and Builders

1. Dreck Spurlock Wilson, *African American Architects: A Biographical Dictionary, 1865–1945* (New York: Routledge, 2004), 140–41.
2. "Farrar & Moore," *Richmond Planet*, December 23, 1893, 3.
3. "Prominent Builder," *Richmond Planet*, December 23, 1983, 3.
4. Hoffman, *Race, Class and Power*, 167.
5. Ibid.
6. "Prominent Builder."
7. Green, et al., *Lost Virginia*, 190.
8. Rachleff, *Black Labor*, 94.
9. Ibid.
10. Ibid., 96.
11. Ann Field Alexander, *Race Man: The Rise and Fall of the "Fighting Editor," John Mitchell, Jr.* (Charlottesville: University of Virginia Press, 2002), 144.
12. Hoffman, *Race, Class and Power*, 152–53.
13. Ibid., 153.
14. Ibid., 154.
15. T. Tyler Potterfield Jr., "John A. Lankford and Charles T. Russell: Architects for Richmond's Black Community, 1900–1920" (unpublished seminar paper, Department of Art History, Virginia Commonwealth University, n.d.), 1.
16. Paul Kelsey Williams, "John Anderson Lankford (1874–1946)" in Wilson, *African American Architects*, 253.
17. Richard R. Wright, *Centennial Encyclopedia of the African Methodist Episcopal Church* (Philadelphia: n.p., 1948), 255.
18. Richard Kevin Dozier, "Tuskegee: Booker T. Washington's Contribution to the Education of Black Architects" (PhD diss., University of Michigan, 1990), 47.
19. Emmett J. Scott, "Training Head and Hand: Architectural and Mechanical Drawing at Tuskegee," quoted in Dozier, "Tuskegee," 56.
20. Israel L. Butt, *History of African Methodism in Virginia or Four Decades in the Old Dominion* (Norfolk, VA: Hampton Institute Press, 1908), 251.
21. John A. Lankford, "Our Stewardship: Report of J.A. Lankford, Supervising Architect of the A.M.E. Church," in *Report of Lankford's Artistic Church and Other Designs* (Washington, D.C.: Hamilton Printing Co., ca. 1924), 11.
22. Ibid.
23. John E. Wells and Robert E. Dalton, *The Virginia Architects, 1835–1955: A Biographical Dictionary* (Richmond: New South Architectural Press, 1997), 245.
24. "Negroes At The Top: Architects Who Have Won Their Way Through Pure Merit," *Richmond Planet*, February 29, 1908, 1.
25. Wright, *Centennial Encyclopedia*, 257.
26. Marlowe, *Grand Mission*, 140.
27. Wright, *Centennial Encyclopedia*, 257.
28. "Rev. Dr. W.L. Taylor's Residence," *Richmond Planet*, August 13, 1910, 1.
29. There are several different dates for the Taylor house: 1904 (Wilson, *Buildings of Virginia*) to 1907 (Wells and Dalton, *The Virginia Architects*). The same article in the *Richmond Planet* that described the house as "palatial" also called it Taylor's "new" residence in 1910.
30. Wilson, *Buildings of Virginia*, 232–233.
31. Butt, *History of African Methodism*, 251.
32. Potterfield, "Lankford and Russell," 3.
33. *Souvenir Views: Negro Enterprises & Residences* (Richmond, VA: n.p., n.d.).

34. "Southern Aid Society Throws Open Her Doors—A Brilliant Affair," *Richmond Planet*, October 3, 1908, 1.

35. Ibid., 1.

36. Paul Kelsey Williams, "John Anderson Lankford (1874–1946)" in Wilson, *African American Architects*, 253.

37. Wright, *Centennial Encyclopedia* 257.

38. Potterfield, "Lankford and Russell," 4.

39. It is noteworthy that the 1895 First Battalion Virginia Volunteers Armory on Leigh Street was not designed with a large space for meetings and drilling. All the other (white) armory buildings in Richmond (several of which were built at the same time) featured a large drill hall. Whether this omission with the Leigh Street Armory is due to budgetary constraints or other reasons is not known, but the fact remains that the design of Richmond's only armory for blacks was atypical of most armory designs.

40. Wells and Dalton, *The Virginia Architects*, 33.

41. Green et al., *Lost Virginia*, 189.

42. "Hon. Marcus Garvey Speaks to Large Audience in Reformers Hall," *Richmond Planet*, July 8, 1922, 1.

43. Green et al., *Lost Virginia*, 189.

44. Ibid., 190.

45. Farrar is given credit for the construction of the Hill mansion under a photograph of the house taken in 1911 that appeared in the *Richmond Planet*. See "Why Did Cashier Hill Leave Richmond?" *Richmond Planet*, April 8, 1911, 1.

46. "Cashier R.T. Hill Disappears," *Richmond Planet*, April 1, 1911, 1.

47. Alexander, *Race Man*, 28.

48. "True Reformers' Bank Closes," *Richmond Planet*, October 29, 1910, 1.

49. Marlowe, *Grand Mission*, 116.

50. Alexander, *Race Man*, 178.

51. "Lynchburg Properties Were Sold," *Richmond Planet*, June 17, 1911, 1.

52. *Richmond Planet*, April 5, 1910, 8.

53. Alexander, *Race Man*, 154–55.

54. "Mechanics' Savings Bank Buys More Broad Street Property," *Richmond Planet*, July 1, 1905, 1.

55. *Souvenir Views*.

56. Ibid.

57. Alexander, *Race Man*, 171.

58. "The New Bank Building," *Richmond Planet*, February 6, 1909, 1.

59. Ibid.

60. "A.M.E. Church to Have Better Supervision of Their Church Edifice," *Richmond Planet*, May 30, 1908, 1.

61. "Mechanics' Savings Bank Building—Front View," *Richmond Planet*, June 12, 1909, 1.

62. "White Property Owners Object. Attempt to Prevent the Erection of the New Bank Building," *Richmond Planet*, July 17, 1909, 1.

63. The collection of architectural drawings that was the product of this procedure is an invaluable resource for students of Richmond's architectural history. See Bureau of Permits and Inspections, building permit architectural blueprints and specifications, 1907–1949, accession number 30150, 30745, 38536, Library of Virginia, Richmond City.

64. *Richmond Times-Dispatch*, July 9, 1909; quoted in "White Property Owners Object. Attempt to Prevent the Erection of the New Bank Building," *Richmond Planet*, July 17, 1909, 1.

65. "Permit is Issued—Building Inspector Beck Could Wait No Longer," *Richmond Planet*, July 24, 1909, 1.

66. *Richmond Times-Dispatch*, July 9, 1909; quoted in "White Property Owners Object."

67. "The New Building," *Richmond Planet*, October 2, 1909, 1.

68. "Mechanics' Savings Bank Opens Its Doors," *Richmond Planet*, July 2, 1910, 1.

69. Alexander, *Race Man*, 173–77.

70. Ibid., 171.

71. O. Jackson Sands, *John Mitchell, Jr.: His Life as Mirrored by the Richmond Planet* (Williamstown, MA: n.p., 1971), 50.

72. See Bureau of Permits and Inspections, building permit architectural blueprints and specifications, 1907–1949, collection 30150, 30745, 38536, control number 1791, Library of Virginia, Richmond City.
73. Alexander, *Race Man*, 103.

5. The New Architects at Work

1. T. Tyler Potterfield Jr., "Charles Thaddeus Russell (1875–1952)," in Wilson, *African American Architects*, 364.
2. Ibid.
3. Charles T. Russell, "Experience Practical and Professional." (Typewritten manuscript, signed by Russell, copy in possession of the author, 1923), 1.
4. Potterfield, "Lankford and Russell," 364.
5. Ibid.
6. Marlowe, *Grand Mission*, 118.
7. "Residence and Apartments to be Built for Lawyer J. Thomas Hewin," Bureau of Permits and Inspections, building permit architectural blueprints and specifications, 1907–1949, control Number 1317, Library of Virginia, Richmond City.
8. Potterfield, "Lankford and Russell," 1.
9. "Confectionary and Ice Cream Saloon," *Richmond Planet*, January 9, 1892, 2.
10. "Office Building for the Richmond Beneficial Insurance Co., N.W. Corner Jackson and Second Sts," Bureau of Permits and Inspections, building permit architectural blueprints and specifications, 1907–1949, control number 2982, Library of Virginia, Richmond City.
11. T. Tyler Potterfield Jr., "Professor Charles T. Russell, 1875–1942: Virginia's Pioneer African-American Architect," in "…And the Walls Came Tumbling Down: A History of African-American Architects in the District of Columbia and Virginia" (unpublished manuscript, 1995), 9.
12. Wilson, *Buildings of Virginia*, 234.
13. "Bank Building for the Richmond Beneficial Insurance Company," Bureau of Permits and Inspections, building permit architectural blueprints and specifications, 1907–1949, control number 236, Library of Virginia, Richmond City. Farrar did on occasion work with a white architect, Carl Ruehrmund, who designed the Mechanics' Savings Bank for John Mitchell Jr. Farrar is also listed as the contractor for Ruehrmund's combination store and apartments constructed in 1912 for the Beneficial Insurance Company at 726 North Second Street. See the microfilm version of the above records (where actual building permit forms are recorded), permit no. 3012, November 6, 1912.
14. Ibid.
15. "First Virginia Volunteers Battalion Armory," Office of City Engineer, Architectural Drawings, Plans, and Plats, 1809–1975, collection 34886ab, folder 1, Library of Virginia, Richmond City.
16. Alexander, *Race Man*, 79.
17. Ibid., 80.
18. "Their Gala Day, Also a Gala Night For the Colored Soldiers," *The State*, October 17, 1895, 1.
19. "The Colored Armory," *Richmond Planet*, October 12, 1895, 1.
20. "New Armory," *Richmond Planet*, October 19, 1895, 4.
21. "Jackson Ward Brevities," *Richmond Planet*, October 19, 1895, 1.
22. For a history of African American militia units in Reconstruction Virginia, see Roger D. Cunningham, "They Are as Proud of Their Uniform As Any Who Serve Virginia: African American Participation in the Virginia Volunteers, 1872–99," *The Virginia Magazine of History and Biography* 110, 3 (2002), 293–338.
23. Shirley L. Callihan et al., *A Mini-History of the Richmond Public Schools—1869–1992* (Richmond: City of Richmond Public School Board, 1992), 136.
24. "Addition to Monroe School for Recreational Purposes," Bureau of Permits and Inspections, building permit architectural blueprints and specifications, 1907–1949, accession number 30150, 30745, 38536, control number 2274, Library of Virginia, Richmond City.
25. Francis Earle Lutz, *Richmond in World War II* (Richmond: The Dietz Press, Inc., 1951), 568.
26. Of the six turreted armories that once stood in Richmond, only two now exist: the First Battalion Virginia Volunteers armory on Leigh Street and the 1909 Blues Armory at Sixth and Marshall Streets. The Black History Museum and Cultural Center of Virginia, which once occupied the armory, is currently located in

the Adolf Dill House at 00 East Clay Street. This 1830 building has housed the headquarters of Maggie Walker's women's club, the Council of Colored Women and later a city library for the residents of Jackson Ward. It continues to serve the African American community as the repository of historic items and reference materials dealing with black culture in Richmond. See Wilson, *Buildings of Virginia*, 235.

27. "Why Pay Rent?" *Richmond Planet*, September 9, 1908, 8.

28. The congregation moved to a new location at 2600 Idlewood Avenue in 1965. An evangelical congregation called the Glorious Church of God in Christ, Number 1, now uses the original church structure.

29. "Church Building for the River View Baptist Church Congregation," Bureau of Permits and Inspections, building permit architectural blueprints and specifications, 1907–1949, control number 643, Library of Virginia, Richmond City.

30. *Negro Baptist Churches in Richmond* (Richmond: Historical Records Survey of Virginia, 1940), 29.

31. George W. Rogers, "Almost Forgotten Strip in Toll Road Line Recalled as Historic 'Postletown," *Richmond News Leader*, November 1, 1955, 12.

32. "St. Luke Building," National Register of Historic Places: Inventory—Nomination Form (Washington, D.C.: United States Department of the Interior, Heritage Conservation and Recreation Service, 1982).

33. Maggie L. Walker, *Fiftieth Anniversary—Golden Jubilee Historical Report of the R.W.G. Council, I.O. St. Luke, 1867–1917* (Richmond: Everett Waddey Co., 1917), 55.

34. Potterfield, "Professor Russell," 7.

35. "C.T. Russell—Experience Practical and Professional," signed curriculum vita (1923) by Russell, copy of manuscript in possession of the author.

36. The cost of remodeling the St. Luke's Building comes from a 1922 picture postcard of the building, in possession of the author.

37. Marlowe, *Grand Mission*, 174.

38. Walker, *Fiftieth Anniversary*.

39. "St. Luke Building."

40. Callihan et al., *Mini-History*, 215–16.

41. "Dedication Today At Walker High," *Richmond News Leader*, June 16, 1937, 4.

42. Callihan et al., *Mini-History*, 215–16.

43. An interesting if oblique parallel to both Maggie Walker and her career as an African American woman entrepreneur can be found in that of Madame C.J. Walker, of Indianapolis, Indiana. Although not related, the two Walkers each established commercial outlets for African Americans, particularly African American women. Madame C.J. Walker was the inventor of what became known as the Walker System of personal care products for blacks, which were sold door-to-door by a network of black saleswomen. By 1910, there were more than five thousand "Walker Agents" selling Madame C.J. Walker beauty products. Both Maggie Walker and Madame C.J. Walker established their headquarters in multiuse buildings specifically commissioned to serve the particular needs of their growing businesses. Both women commissioned African American architects to build (or in Maggie Walker's case, redesign) their personal residences. The story of these two African American women is remarkably similar, and they shared a passion for black economic self-determination in the early 1900s. Both Walkers participated in a project to preserve Frederick Douglass's home as a memorial to the pioneering black leader. They also shared a philosophy regarding the power of architecture, using their respective homes and businesses as demonstrations of the potential of black-owned enterprise and as a call to achievement for people of color.

44. Abigail Adams National Bancorp acquired Consolidated Bank & Trust Company, the direct successor to Maggie Walker's St. Luke Bank, in 2005. See "Bank Merger OK'd," *Richmond Free Press*, June 30–July 2, 2005, 1.

45. "Historic House Has New Owner," *Richmond Times-Dispatch*, July 16, 1979, B4.

46. Wilson, *Buildings of Virginia*, 233–34.

47. "Quality Row" historical marker placed by the National Park Service at the Maggie L. Walker National Site.

48. Michael A. Plater, *African-American Entrepreneurship in Richmond, 1890–1940* (New York: Garland, 1996), 6.

49. Ibid., 9.

50. Potterfield, "Professor Russell," 10.

51. Information about the Hughes house was provided by the Alliance to Conserve Old Richmond Neighborhoods. At the time of this writing, ACORN was promoting the sale of the Hughes house to a renovator or developer who would be sensitive to the building's importance to African American history. See also Potterfield, "Lankford and Russell."

52. "Plan of Brick Building to be Used as a Restaurant, David R. Cross, Owner," Bureau of Permits and Inspections, building permit architectural blueprints and specifications, 1907–1949, control number 3085, Library of Virginia, Richmond City.

53. Ophelia Johnson, "Hidden History," *Richmond Times-Dispatch*, May 3, 1994, G1.

54. Richard A. Singletary, "Harvey Nathaniel Johnson, Sr. (1892–1973)," in Wilson, *Buildings of Virginia*, 237.

55. "Johnson Built Historic Buildings and a Loving Reputation," *Virginian Pilot*, October 16, 1994, J3.

56. Singletary, "Harvey Johnson," 238–39.

57. Ibid., 241.

58. Elizabeth Dementi and Wayne Dementi, eds., *Celebrate Richmond Theater* (Richmond: Dietz Press, 1999), 86.

59. "Terminal Station for the Richmond and Rappahannock Railway Company," Bureau of Permits and Inspections, building permit architectural blueprints and specifications, 1907–1949, control number 131, Library of Virginia, Richmond City. See also Thomas Dill, "Steamships, Trains, and 'Jolly Trolleys': Virginia and the Baltimore Trade," *Virginia Cavalcade* 36, 4 (Spring 1987).

60. Susan Gergen Horner, "Ethel Madison Bailey Furman (1893–1976)," in Wilson, *African American Architects*, 163.

61. Jessica Breeden, "Ethel Bailey Furman" (lecture, Fourth Baptist Church, Richmond, VA, April 16, 1997). Photocopy of lecture notes.

62. *Negro Baptist Churches*, 18.

63. Horner, "Ethel Furman," 164.

64. Ibid., 163.

65. Ibid., 162–63.

6. Virginia Union University and Frederick Douglass Court

1. Dr. Raymond P. Hylton, "University History," Virginia Union University, http://www.vuu.edu/aboutvuu/history.htm.

2. Wells and Dalton, *Virginia Architects*, 99.

3. William Lebovich, "Albert Irvin Cassell (1895–1969)," in Wilson, *African American Architects*, 91–94.

4. T. Tyler Potterfield Jr., "Charles Thaddeus Russell (1875–1952)," in Wilson, *African American Architects*, 364.

5. City of Richmond, Department of Public Safety, Bureau of Building Inspection, permit no. 16843, July 1, 1926, 10.

6. Wells and Dalton, *Virginia Architects*, 396.

7. The various components of this complex of buildings have different official names: the gymnasium-auditorium is named Barco-Stevens Hall, the tower of the Belgian Building is the Vann Tower and another part of the building is the William J. Clark Hall.

8. Potterfield, "Charles Russell," 365.

9. "Regarding Home Building," *Richmond Planet*, April 29, 1905, 2.

10. "The Modern Home," *Richmond Planet*, April 29, 1905, 2.

11. "Colored Folks Buying Property," *Richmond Planet*, December 3, 1904, 1.

12. "Property for Sale," *Richmond Planet*, November 25, 1905, 1.

13. Hoffman, *Race, Class and Power*, 159.

14. Ibid., 175–76.

15. Ibid., 171.

16. "Happy Woodville is the Colored Man's Paradise," *Richmond Planet*, May 5, 1906, 8.

17. Marlowe, *Grand Mission*, 185.

18. An interesting example of an African American real estate development outside Richmond was "Brownville," located west of the city. In 1898 the Grand Fountain of the United Order of True Reformers purchased 634 acres on which it established an "Old Folks Home" and sold lots on the adjacent property. As one historian wrote, "The United Order of the True Reformers not only facilitated the physical expansion of the black community into areas of the city already built up by whites, but provided the means for the city's blacks to participate in the expansion and growth of Richmond into the surrounding countryside." See Hoffman, *Race, Class and Power*, 155–56.
19. Howard Road or Street is seen as forming one of the boundaries of Frederick Douglass Court on the original plat, but was renamed Overbrook Road.
20. Charles Louis Knight, *Negro Housing in Certain Virginia Cities* (Richmond: William Byrd Press, 1927), 122.
21. Ibid.
22. Marlowe, *Grand Mission*, 185.
23. Knight, *Negro Housing*, 123.
24. Entry for "Robinson" in *The African American Almanac*, 8th ed. (Detroit, MI: Gale Group, 2000), 487.
25. Much of the anecdotal information about Robinson was obtained from Mrs. Kathryn Reid, interviewed on April 28, 2005. Mrs. Reid and her late husband, Leon, were friends of the Robinsons and knew Justice Robinson for many years.
26. Elvatrice Parker Belsches, *Richmond, Virginia* (Chicago: Arcadia Publishing, 2002), 81.
27. The other date on the cornerstone, 1902, probably marks the year the Richmond Hospital and Training School for Nurses was established by Dr. Sara G. Jones. Dr. Jones, the daughter of a Richmond building contractor, was among the first African Americans in Virginia to pass the medical board exams. See Belsches, *Richmond, Virginia*, 78.
28. Mrs. Kathryn Reid, interview on April 24, 2005.
29. Potterfield, "Lankford and Russell."
30. Ibid.
31. Marlowe, *Grand Mission*, 220.
32. "Brick Residence in Douglass Court for Mr. W.A. Jordan," Bureau of Permits and Inspections, building permit architectural blueprints and specifications, 1907–1949, control number 1436, Library of Virginia, Richmond City.
33. "A Rezoning Move to Be Defeated," *Richmond News Leader*, February 23, 1953, 10.
34. Ibid.
35. Ibid.
36. Ibid.
37. Ibid.
38. Mrs. Kathryn Reid, interview on April 24, 2005.
39. Ibid.

7. Highways and Expressways

1. "Fay Heads City's Slum Clearance Program; New Surveys Set," *Richmond News Leader*, October 25, 1950, 1.
2. Mordecai, *By-Gone Days*, 288.
3. As a gauge of the steep hillside that surrounded Navy Hill, a history of the 1952 addition to the south side of the Navy Hill School notes that an additional expenditure of $35,000 was added for piling that had to be extended down sixty-five feet through fill in order to find a firm footing for the building. See Callihan et al., *Mini-History*, 142.
4. The neighborhood that was planned for this ridge was named in honor of the naval battles of the War of 1812. The houses built there had a fine view of the surrounding wooded valley. See Mordecai, *By-Gone Days*, 288.
5. Scott, *Old Richmond Neighborhoods*, 283.
6. Ibid., 284.

7. *Annual Report of the City Engineer of Richmond, Virginia, for the Year Ending December 31, 1892* (Richmond: Everett Waddey Co., City Printers, 1893), 8.

8. The Navy Hill and Fulton Schools were very similar in design and decoration to the Moore Street School (1887), which still exists as the rear wing of Carver School on Leigh Street. For plans of Navy Hill School see the City Engineer's Office Collection, Architectural Drawings and Plans, folder 82, Library of Virginia, Richmond City.

9. Alexander, *Race Man*, 11.

10. Ibid, 17.

11. Ibid, 11.

12. Marlowe, *Grand Mission*, 7.

13. Maggie L. Walker, "Reunion of Old Pupils," July 29, 1906, Leigh Street Methodist Church, Addresses, 1909. As quoted in Marlowe, *Grand Mission*, 7.

14. Alexander, *Race Man*, 78–79.

15. Callihan et al., *Mini-History*, 142.

16. Stonewall Jackson School (formerly West End School) at 1520 West Main Street was built in 1887 and, although it has been converted into offices, it remains one of the best-preserved Italianate Richmond school buildings of the period. It retains its original decoration and is probably very similar to the appearance of the interiors of Navy Hill and Fulton Schools.

17. For an illustration of the Civil War–era buildings that served as Navy Hill School, see "New Navy Hill School," *Frank Leslie's Illustrated Newspaper*, July 21, 1883, 1.

18. Scott, *Old Richmond Neighborhoods*, 279–84.

19. Ibid., 284.

20. Callihan et al., *Mini-History*, 142.

21. "Ex-Navy Hill Residents Come Back," *Richmond Times-Dispatch*, July 18, 1993, B7.

22. "Road Forces School Closing—Navy Hill in Its Last Week," *Richmond News Leader*, September 14, 1965, 17.

23. "10% of Negroes in City Evicted for Projects," *Richmond Times-Dispatch*, May 19, 1957, D1.

24. Ibid.

25. Ibid.

26. Callihan et al., *Mini-History*, 143.

27. "Ex-Navy Hill Residents," B7.

28. *Negro Baptist Churches*, 24.

29. Kimball, *American City*, 76.

30. Benjamin Ross, historian of Sixth Mt. Zion Baptist Church, interview on September 4, 2006. The acquisition of the former Lutheran church owned by a German congregation in Jackson Ward is emblematic of the change from the early German-speaking demographic of the neighborhood to an African American population for which the area is currently known.

31. *Negro Baptist Churches*, 24.

32. "Brick Church for Fifth Street Baptist Church," Bureau of Permits and Inspections, building permit architectural blueprints and specifications, 1907–1949, control number 1389, Library of Virginia, Richmond City. The large number of designs created and constructed by Davis Brothers in this collection testifies to their influence on building in Richmond in the years before World War II.

33. "Church Seeks North Side Site," *Richmond Times-Dispatch*, February 20, 1975.

34. "Group Opposing Move of Church," *Richmond News Leader*, March 29, 1975, 13.

35. "Long Controversy Ended, Baptist Church Building is Vacant," *Richmond Afro-American*, June 7, 1980, 2.

36. Ibid.

8. Urban Destruction as Urban Renewal

1. "Building lots in the town of Fulton," *Daily Richmond Times*, April 14, 1853, 2.

2. "Resident of Same Block of 'Fulton' For 78 Years Recalls Incidents of Past," *Richmond News Leader*, March 27, 1936, 11.

3. Callihan et al., *Mini-History*, 68.

4. Ibid., 69.

5. "'Birthplace of Richmond' Now Appears Sick, Shaggy," *Richmond Times-Dispatch*, January 1, 1967, B1.

6. Ibid.

7. Scott C. Davis, *The World of Patience Gromes: Making and Unmaking a Black Community* (Lexington: University Press of Kentucky, 1988), 115.

8. "Fulton: Community Sprit Grows in Ailing Area of City," *Richmond Times-Dispatch*, February 9, 1969, F1.

9. Ibid.

10. "Vacant Promises Hover Over Empty Lots in Fulton," *Richmond News Leader*, August 10, 1988, 17.

11. "Fulton Renewal Plan," *Richmond Times-Dispatch*, February 4, 1969, B1.

12. "Fulton: Community Sprit Grows in Ailing Area of City," *Richmond Times-Dispatch*, February 9, 1969, F1.

13. Ibid.

14. Ibid.

15. "Fulton Area—Plan Recommended for Redevelopment," *Richmond Times-Dispatch*, February 4, 1969, A1.

16. "Fulton Group Airs Its Renewal Plan," *Richmond Times-Dispatch*, November 21, 1968.

17. "Fulton: Community Sprit Grows in Ailing Area of City," *Richmond Times-Dispatch*, February 9, 1969, F1.

18. Ibid.

19. "Fulton Residents Exhibited Spirit," *Richmond News Leader*, July 20, 1983, 1.

20. "Vacant Promises Hover Over Empty Lots in Fulton," *Richmond News Leader*, August 10, 1988, 17.

21. Davis, *Patience Gromes*, 197.

22. Ibid., 211.

23. Callihan et al., *Mini-History*, 68.

24. The Historical Records Survey of Virginia, Division of Professional and Service Projects, Works Projects Administration, "Negro Baptist Churches in Richmond," in *Inventory of the Church Archives of Virginia* (Richmond: Historical Records Survey of Virginia, 1940), 34.

25. Ibid., 25.

26. "The New and the Old," *Richmond Afro-American*, October 8, 1977, B12.

27. "Fulton Roots—Long-Dead Indian Returns, Guards His Heritage," *Richmond News Leader*, November 19, 1971, B1.

28. Ibid.

29. Ibid.

30. Ibid.

31. "Fulton Plan Sparks 'Roots' Fight," *Richmond Times-Dispatch*, November 20, 1977, C2.

32. Ibid.

33. "Taking Bites," *Richmond News Leader*, March 2, 1978, 12.

34. "Fulton: Populated More By a Spirit Than People," *Richmond Times-Dispatch*, September 21, 1980, H1.

35. "Fulton Pair Facing Move Win Order," *Richmond Times-Dispatch*, September 26, 1980, B4.

36. "Landmarks Unit to Study Value of Fulton Homes," *Richmond News Leader*, October 3, 1980, 3.

37. "Landmark Unit Rejects Fulton Bid," *Richmond Times-Dispatch*, October 22, 1980, D4.

38. "Warriner Blasts Fulton Project," *Richmond Times-Dispatch*, October 25, 1980, B1.

39. Ibid.

40. Ibid.

41. Ibid.

42. "What Became of Fulton?" *Richmond Afro-American*, October 4, 1980, 11.

9. A Community Saved

1. See Howard H. Harlan, *Zion-Town—A Study in Human Ecology* (Charlottesville: Publications of the University of Virginia Phelps-Stokes Fellowship Papers, Number Thirteen, 1935).

2. Elsa Barkley Brown and Gregg D. Kimball, "Mapping the Terrain of Black Richmond," *Journal of Urban History* 21, 3 (March 1995), 303–04.

3. Ibid., 304.

4. "Church History" (unpublished pamphlet, Westwood Baptist Church, n.d.).

5. Ibid.

6. Henrico County Deed Book 98, 66.

7. The frame building was covered with brick veneer in 1977 and still exists inside the present building complex. See Office of the Assessor of Real Estate (microfilm), reel 678, W20-65-016, Library of Virginia, Richmond City.

8. Jean Curtis, interview on October 8, 2003.

9. Mary Thompson Parks, *"Forget Me Nots:" Memories of Rio Vista Virginia by Mary Thompson Parks* (Richmond: Old Dominion Press, n.d.).

10. Curtis, interview.

11. Callihan et al., *Mini-History*, 225.

12. Hoffman, *Race, Class and Power*, 96–97.

13. "Water, Water Aplenty But Little for Drinking In Westwood Village," *Richmond News Leader*, February 19, 1947, 1.

14. "Health Menace at Westwood," *Richmond News Leader*, July 17, 1945, 3.

15. "Aldermen Deny Sanitary Steps At Westwood," *Richmond News Leader*, July 11, 1945, 3.

16. "Council Gets Modified Version of Proposed Westwood Park," *Richmond Times-Dispatch*, January 8, 1946, 6.

17. Ibid.

18. "Westhampton Park Proposal Is Tabled," *Richmond Times-Dispatch*, April 16, 1946, 6.

19. "Clashing Stands Are Voiced at Mass Meeting On Proposal To Demolish Westwood Village," *Richmond Times-Dispatch*, April 5, 1947, 4.

20. "Most Unpleasant Public Duties," *Richmond News Leader*, February 20, 1947, 12.

21. "Mass Meeting Held on Plan for Westwood," *Richmond Times-Dispatch*, April 5, 1947.

22. "Clashing Stands Are Voiced at Mass Meeting On Proposal To Demolish Westwood Village," *Richmond Times-Dispatch*, April 5, 1947, 1.

23. Ibid.

24. Ibid.

25. Ibid.

26. "Westwood—Touchstone for Richmond," *Richmond Times-Dispatch*, April 6, 1947, 2D.

27. "Voice of the People," *Richmond Times-Dispatch*, April 8, 1947, 10.

28. Ibid.

29. "Pastor Says Westwood Will Pay—Residents to Accept Offer of Utilities," *Richmond News Leader*, April 30, 1947, 1.

30. Ibid.

31. "3 Negroes Apply In Westhampton," *Richmond News Leader*, July 24, 1958, 1.

32. Ibid.

33. Ibid.

34. "Some Not So Ancient History," *Richmond News Leader*, July 25, 1958, 10.

35. Arthur Ashe, *Days of Grace* (New York: Random House, 1993), 333.

36. Ibid.

37. In January 2000 the residents of Westwood again rallied behind the minister of Westwood Baptist Church in opposition to a branch of the Bank of Richmond that was proposed for the corner of Patterson Avenue and Dunbar Street, once the site of the community's single sanitary water hydrant and the symbol of the maltreatment of the neighborhood by the city of Richmond. Led by Reverend Linda D. Stevens, residents strongly objected to the proposed bank and accused Councilman John Conrad of a conflict of interest since he was one of the founders of the bank. Among those who appeared at the meeting in support of the Bank of Richmond was Senator Henry L. Marsh III, Richmond's first black mayor. With Conrad sitting silently throughout the meeting and finally abstaining on the vote, the measure to approve placement of the new Bank of Richmond branch on the edge of Westwood passed

eight to zero. See "Council Approves Bank's Plan Over Residents' Objections," *Richmond Times-Dispatch*, January 25, 2000, B1.

10. The City's Black Churches

1. "An Old Landmark," *Harper's Weekly*, June 27, 1874, 545.
2. Charles F. Irons, "And All These Things Shall Be Added Unto You: The First African Baptist Church, Richmond, 1841–1865," *Virginia Cavalcade* (Winter 1998), 35.
3. "An Old Landmark," 545.
4. Wilson, *Buildings of Virginia*, 184.
5. Wells and Dalton, *Virginia Architects*, 111.
6. David R. Goldfield, "Black Life in Old South Cities," in Edward D.C. Campbell Jr. and Kym S. Rice, eds., *Before Freedom Came: African-American Life in the Antebellum South* (Richmond and Charlottesville: Museum of the Confederacy and the University Press of Virginia, 1991), 144.
7. William H. Chafe, Raymond Gavins, Robert Korstad, et al., *Remembering Jim Crow: African Americans Tell About Life in the Segregated South* (New York: New Press, 2001), 90.
8. *50 Years' History of Sixth Mount Zion Baptist Church, Richmond, Virginia* (Richmond: John Mitchell Jr., 1917), 9.
9. Ibid., 4.
10. Mary Wingfield Scott describes this migration into Jackson Ward: "Within twenty years [1866], Negroes began to move east on Duval, and in the seventies the street was permanently colored." See *Old Richmond Neighborhoods*, 258.
11. Richard A. Singletary, "Five Nineteenth-Century African-American Churches in Richmond, Virginia," in *Styles of Virginia Architecture: New Findings from the Department of Art History, School of the Arts, Virginia Commonwealth University, Abstracts of the Fourth Annual Architectural History Symposium* (Richmond: Eye in Hand, 1996), 20.
12. "The Dedication of the Sixth Mount Zion Baptist Church—A Costly Edifice," *Richmond Planet*, May 31, 1890, 1.
13. Ibid.
14. Ibid.
15. Janet Caggiano, "Moving Words," *Richmond Times-Dispatch*, April 12, 2005, D1.
16. "I. Lincoln Bailey, General Contractor and Builder of the Sixth Mt. Zion Baptist Church, Richmond, Va." (undated advertisement, source unknown).
17. Elizabeth Dementi and Wayne Dementi, eds., *Celebrate Richmond* (Richmond: Dietz Press, 1999), 147.
18. Francis Merrill Foster, "Catholic School Filled Educational Needs of Blacks," in Earle Dunford, ed., *I Remember When: A Series Reprinted from the Richmond Times-Dispatch* (N.p., 1989), 29.
19. "Van de Vyver College," *Richmond Planet*, September 30, 1911, 1.
20. "Van De Vyver School for Colored Pupils," Bureau of Permits and Inspections, building permit architectural blueprints and specifications, 1907–1949, control number 207, Library of Virginia, Richmond City.
21. "Van de Vyver College," 1.
22. Ibid.
23. Foster, "Catholic School," 29.
24. Kimball, *American City*, 261.
25. *Negro Baptist Churches*, 17.
26. Donald R. Traser, *The Organ in Richmond: A History of the Organs, Organists, and Organ Music in Richmond, Virginia, from 1816 to 2001* (Richmond: Richmond Chapter, American Guild of Organists, 2001), 21.
27. The story of Beck's changing the Richmond skyline by condemnation of many historic church steeples can be found in a scrapbook of clippings the building inspector kept during his career. See Office of Building Inspection, Scrapbook, 1908–1920, accession 37278 microfilm reel 465, Library of Virginia, Richmond City.
28. Charles T. Russell, "Experience Practical and Professional" (typewritten ms. signed by Russell, 1923), 2. Copy in possession of the author.

29. Among the congregations credited to Ebenezer Baptist Church in Richmond are Shiloah Baptist Church (now Cedar Street Baptist Church), St. John's Baptist Church, Mt. Carmel Baptist Church, Riverview Baptist Church, Mt. Vernon Baptist Church and Pleasant Grove Baptist Church in Ellerson, Virginia. See *Negro Baptist Churches*, 17.

30. The term "slab building" may refer to what was known as the 1797 "Old Plank Church," which a history of Central Methodist Church locates at Tenth and Perry Streets. See Frank B. Dunford, *History of Central Methodist Church, Fourteenth and Porter Streets, Richmond, Virginia* (Richmond: W.M. Brown & Son, 1942), 10.

31. William Lee Ransome, *History of the First Baptist Church, South Richmond* (Richmond: First Baptist Church, South Richmond, n.d.)., 24.

32. Benjamin B. Weisiger III, *Old Manchester & Its Environs, 1769–1910* (Richmond: William Byrd Press, 1993), 17.

33. Ransome, *History*, 25.

34. Ibid., 24.

35. Ibid., 27.

36. Laverne Byrd Smith, *Traveling On…First Baptist, South Richmond. The 133-Year Journey after the Civil War: The Wells, Ransome, Jones Years 1865–1998, Vol. II* (Richmond: Northlight Publishing, 1999), 106.

37. Ibid., 107.

38. "The Progress in Manchester—Rev. Binga's Efforts," *Richmond Planet*, November 19, 1892, 1.

39. W. Asbury Christian, *Richmond: Her Past and Present* (Richmond: L.H. Jenkins, 1912), 454.

40. Ransome, *History*, 38.

41. Ibid., 51–52.

42. Ibid., 52.

43. Ibid.

44. Ibid.

45. Ibid., 53–58.

46. Smith, *Traveling On*, 365.

47. Termed "Newtown South" so as not to be confused with another historically African American neighborhood called Newtown, west of Jackson Ward.

48. Theresa Evens, "Newtown," in Smith, *Traveling On*, 368.

49. Weisiger, *Old Manchester*, 31.

50. Evens, "Newtown," 368.

51. Ibid.

11. Richmond's African American Cemeteries

1. Veronica A. Davis, *Here I Lay My Burdens Down: A History of the Black Cemeteries of Richmond, Virginia* (Richmond: Dietz Press, 2003), ix. Much of the factual information in this chapter is from Davis's study.

2. State Highway Historical Marker SA-66, "The Execution of Gabriel."

3. Frederick Law Olmsted, *The Cotton Kingdom: A Traveler's Observations on Cotton and Slavery in the American Slave States* (New York: Alfred A. Knopf, 1953), 35.

4. Ibid., 36.

5. Davis, *Here I Lay*, 13.

6. Ibid., 38–39.

7. Moses Bradford's stone does not give any information about him other than his name and unit. Research is continuing at the National Archives about this veteran whose last resting place is this abandoned cemetery. To date, inquiries about Bradford have yielded only the date of his death and the fact that in 1899 he unsuccessfully applied for a disability pension. Information courtesy of Roger Cunningham, military historian, who is leading the Branford research.

8. Gravel Hill Baptist Church was established soon after the Civil War to serve African Americans living in this part of what was then Chesterfield County. Many stories among the congregation confirm the connection between the church and the nearby granite quarries and also the relationship of the church to the abandoned cemetery at the bottom of Granite Hill Road. Information from a conversation with the pastor of Granite Hill Baptist Church, the Reverend Louis G. Jones, April 13, 2005.

9. Gregg Kimball and Nancy Jawish Rives, "To Live in the Hearts We Leave Behind is Not to Die—The Barton Heights Cemeteries of Richmond," *Virginia Cavalcade* (Winter 1997), 118.

10. The area eventually included Sons and Daughters of Ham, Cedarwood, Union Mechanics, Methodist, Ebenzer and Sycamore Cemeteries. Kimball and Rives, "To Live in the Hearts," 130.

11. Davis, *Here I Lay*, 48.

12. "Councilmen Will be Pleased," *Richmond News Leader*, August 3, 1934, 8.

13. "Will Condemn Old Burial Lot—Commission Named by Judge Ingram to Appraise Property," *Richmond News Leader*, December 27, 1934, 10.

14. Davis, *Here I Lay*, 41.

15. Much of the credit for saving the Barton Heights Cemeteries goes to Denise Lester, founder of the Burial Ground Society. Lester campaigned tirelessly for the stabilization, fencing and preservation of the cemetery. May 28, 2002, was proclaimed Denise Lester Day by the city of Richmond in recognition of her efforts in saving this important component of African American history in Richmond. See Davis, *Here I Lay*, 41.

16. Alexander, *Race Man*, 182.

17. Ibid., 190.

18. Davis, *Here I Lay*, 34.

19. Marlowe, *Grand Mission*, 251–52.

20. "Officials are Considering Moving Maggie Walker's Remains," *Richmond News Leader*, June 23, 1984, 7.

21. "Uneven Upkeep Brings Grief at City Cemeteries," *Richmond News Leader*, June 22, 1984.

22. Davis, *Here I Lay*, 50.

23. Ibid., 45–46.

24. Andrew Jacobs, "Histories Vanish Along With South's Cemeteries," *New York Times*, February 8, 2004, A1.

Index

INDEX

www.ingramcontent.com/pod-product-compliance
Lightning Source LLC
Chambersburg PA
CBHW080925100426
42812CB00007B/2372